Charles Wilson
176, Muirfield Drive
Gloucester
Fife. KY6 2PX.

THE ROOF OF ENGLAND

A. H. GRIFFIN

THE ROOF OF ENGLAND

I will go back to the hills again
That are sisters to the sea,
The bare hills, the brown hills,
That stand eternally,
And their strength shall be my strength
And their joy my joy shall be.

Anon

Photographs by G. V. Berry

ROBERT HALE · LONDON

914.28
4

First edition February 1968
Reprinted May 1968
Reprinted July 1970

Robert Hale & Company
63 Old Brompton Road
*London, S.W.*7

SBN 7091 0123 6

3117

Printed in Great Britain
by Ebenezer Baylis and Son Limited
The Trinity Press, Worcester, and London

CONTENTS

ILLUSTRATIONS

In memory of
MY FATHER
who took me up my first hill

FOREWORD

THIS IS not a guide-book. If you want to find the way up
Helvellyn or Scafell Pike you must look elsewhere; there's no
lack of information. Better still, study your map and work it
out for yourself. No, this is not a book for the rucksack, but
rather for the bookshelf or perhaps the bedside table. It is, I
hope, a book for people who love the Lake District and especially its mountains, whether they walk the ridges or climb the
crags or remember the hills from younger days or admire them
from the dales. A book for people who think that hills are
important.

I'm not sure how many mountains there are in the Lake
District for I'm never very clear exactly what a mountain is.
Hills 3,000 feet high wouldn't be called mountains in Switzerland or Kashmir, but Scafell in winter is a mountain to me.
Perhaps you could say there are scores of mountains in the Lake
District but 'fells' is a better word, and in this book I have
attempted personal portraits of fifty of them, including some
groups of hills. Obviously, many have had to be left out, but the
most interesting have been included. Perhaps I might have
given a separate portrait of Haystacks, a magnificent little
mountain, and at one time Pike o'Blisco was going in—until I
realized I had been almost over-generous with Langdale. Grisedale Pike would have been included if Hopegill Head had been
left out, and I thought about Haycock, too, but in the end it
disappeared. Fifty seemed a suitable number, and I don't think
there are many, if any, notable omissions.

None of the hills were ascended with the book in mind,
except perhaps for Yewbarrow which I went up while writing
the book, since I hadn't been on the top for years. All the others
have been recollected within the quiet of a study that commands
most of the southern fells and these recollections go back for
much more than forty years. It has been a great joy thinking

back to carefree days when the only things that really mattered were mountains.

With the book in mind I began a monthly series, 'Portraits of Mountains' in the splendid little Lakeland magazine *Cumbria* in April 1962 and these chapters have been based on the series. All have been re-written and a great deal of new matter has been added, but I am very grateful indeed to Mr. Harry Scott, the Editor of *Cumbria*, for his ready co-operation and encouragement over many years.

I am also grateful to Mr. G. V. Berry, the secretary of the Friends of the Lake District, for the magnificent mountain portraits that adorn the book, and to my wife for her long hours of patient labour with typewriter and proofs.

A.H.G.

Cunswick End
near Kendal

WHERE THE RAVENS FLY

THE highest land in England lies in the magical north-west corner we call the Lake District. Here, in sight of the sea and the border hills of Scotland, is the fell country, a smiling land of smoothly shaped dales guarded by blue evening hills where the ravens fly.

These are not big mountains—an active man might climb a dozen in a day—but neither are they merely uplifted lumps of land. Almost without exception, they are hills of character, and as we walk the heights or swarm up the crags or merely watch from the dales how the sunlight, the mists, the snow or the cloud shadows seem to alter their shape and appeal, we come to realize that each fell has its own personality. Most are friendly hills but some, even in sunlight, may have a hidden menace. Some are challenging, some shy; some parade their charms boldly, others hide them; some are lonely, others are often crowded; some are aggressive, some savage, some queenly, some shapely, some almost ugly; all are different. Some have histories going back to the days before history, but others are almost unknown. Some may be ascended by grandmothers and toddlers, but on some of the crags there are climbing routes as difficult as the hardest in the Alps.

And these hills are not just places for the walker or gymnast. On their slopes are lovely tarns, ravines, waterfalls, dancing becks, age-old tracks, woodlands, ancient settlements, the remains of old mines, modern quarries, Forestry Commission plantations and a hundred and one other points of interest. There are the sheep, the birds, the foxes, the Fell ponies, the red deer, the trees, the flowers, the old stone walls, and the way of life of the shepherd, the hunter, the woodsman and the quarryman. All these are part of the mountains. All help to make up the portrait.

People have been going up into these hills for pleasure for

perhaps two hundred years or less, but men have been working up there for at least two thousand years. Indeed, men were chipping stone axes high up in the Langdale Pikes four thousand years ago. And we can go into the hills a hundred times and not find out the whole story.

There is no more exciting land in England than these lonely fells where the ravens fly. These are mountains that change with the seasons, and can change in half an hour. They can be mountains of tragedy, and each year they take their toll of the foolish and the inexperienced. But if you respect them they will always welcome you back with open arms. For me they will always be friendly fells. For thousands, the best place to be, on the right sort of day, with the wind in your hair, is atop the roof of England.

1

THE HILLS OF YOUTH

(Around Coniston)

Coniston Old Man

CONISTON OLD MAN must have been my first two-thousander—a
lone ascent by a small boy in short trousers and town shoes after
a twenty-miles cycle ride. I went up from Torver because it
looked the shortest way and scrambled to the top by way of the
old quarries on the west side above Cove Bridge. Looking back
on this early walk after a lifetime of mountain adventure I can't
recall a single incident of the day except that I remember feeling
very tired on the long ride back. What had prompted me to
tackle this longish day for a youngster I can't say; perhaps I'd
been trying out a new bike. Before that my highest hill had been
Black Combe.

The Old Man rules kindly over his attendant fells and the
Alpine village at his feet like a benign grandfather presiding in
his chimney corner—the highest mountain in Lancashire and
one of the most popular in Lakeland. A venerable and dignified
hump, you might say, and modest too, since he does not lord
it over his vassals from the centre, but merely from the end of
one of his ridges, often looks less impressive than some of his
neighbours, and, indeed, only tops the highest of them by a
paltry three feet. But, retiring and long-suffering as he undoubtedly is, the Old Man is still Coniston's own mountain and
king of the Furness Fells, a mountain hoary with antiquity,
steeped in tradition and inextricably tied up with the affairs of
men since the days before history began.

We view him from afar with deep devotion. "The Old Man's

got his cap on," we say of the cloud-wreath across his summit. "It'll rain before the day's out." Always "the Old Man", for he's always seemed one of us.

No Lake District mountain I can name has been more tunnelled into, gouged out, mined, holed, pitted, pockmarked and generally knocked about than dear old Coniston Old Man but he's still a grand mountain for all the desecration. For perhaps up to two thousand years—until comparatively recent times— men have been digging deep into his heart for his mineral wealth, particularly copper, and during the last two hundred years or so they have been quarrying the slate, sea-green or grey, of which he is made. So that the Old Man is ringed and dotted with tunnels, shafts, holes, caves and spoil-heaps and every day men are high up on his shoulders, banging away with explosives, picks and shovels and gnawing at his vitals.

But although his flesh has been torn, and his very bones exposed, the Old Man displays his honourable scars as a veteran shows off his medals and takes pride in his still youthful vigour. His shape is still unimpaired and from his summit the views are completely individualistic and different than those from any other mountain-top in Lakeland. On the one hand there is a vast seascape, embracing the Isle of Man, with the Furness peninsula and its estuaries in the middle distance and, on the other, the whole, long line of the Scafell group, the highest land in England. In between, there is the quietly wooded length of Coniston Water and several tarns, a peep into the pastoral beauty of southern Lakeland and, straight down below your feet on the north-eastern side, the craggy drop to Low Water and the scattered desolation of the Mines Valley. While on his western slopes, by walking a few steps down from the summit, you will see, facing you across the black pool of Goats Water, the splendid cathedral-like architecture of Dow Crag, one of the finest precipices in the country.

I have known the Old Man intimately since the 1920s when I first went up as a small boy, but for years before that I had known his shape, a friendly, rounded cone on the horizon with the knobbly wrinkles of Walna Scar to his left and the gentler contours of Wetherlam on the other side. Since those early days I've been on his slopes on scores of occasions, most often climbing on Dow Crag, but also scrambling on the lesser crags and boulders scattered about his flanks, exploring the old shafts and tunnels, looking for copper veins and garnet stones in the quarry rocks, bathing in and skating on his tarns, and cutting up

Dow Crag and Coniston Old Man

ice-filled gullies in the winter-time. I've slept in crude huts on his slopes, traced the sheep-trods across his shoulders, watched the birds and sought out the flowers, seen ice-floes half as big as a house on Low Water, fought my way through blizzards to find twelve feet of snow near the summit and slept by the tumbled cairn in an August heat-wave. But no matter what we did in these peaceful hills of my youth we nearly always went back home over the top of the Old Man, because it was the thing to do. I suppose I must have been up there much more than a hundred times.

There's so much to do and see on and around the Old Man. You could spend a month exploring the quarries and not read the whole story, and—if you are adventurously inclined and have some potholing skill—there's enough excitement to last a whole summer in the tunnels and mine workings. Then there's the stone circle south of the Walna Scar track—how many people know it?—the grave of Charmer, the Coniston foxhound killed early this century in a fall from Dow Crag, the curious water-courses and mill-races (one of them seems to be going uphill), the ruined remains of a civilization of thousands of years ago, including perhaps a Bronze Age cemetery, caves by the dozen and boulders by the score (including the famous Pudding Stone, a much more interesting lump of rock than the commercialized and tourist-ridden Bowder Stone).

One of my most interesting possessions is a photograph taken by a Coniston doctor's son several years ago of what he claimed was a flying saucer on Little Arrow Moor, the south-facing slopes of the Old Man. He told me at the time how he watched it come down not far from where men lived in stone huts and caves in the days before recorded history, and described, clearly and factually, exactly what he saw. He'd had no time to open out the bellows of the camera properly and so the picture is blurred, but you can see the unmistakable flying-saucer shape with port-holes as clearly as if he'd photographed a model. But he hadn't, and I still do not know the explanation. Perhaps the Old Man *is* a mystery mountain. Certainly members of the Aetherius Society think so and used to go up there regularly for services near a flat slab of rock between the summit and Brim Fell. They believe the mountain has special properties and is one of several in this country charged with spiritual energy, but I am not competent to discuss these matters.

Another interesting photograph shows my son, then aged four and a half years, and my father standing together at the
2

Wetherlam and Yew Tree Farm

summit cairn. The leader of this two-man expedition—I was not there—had been my son and he carried the camera-case round his shoulder as a sort of guide's badge of office. He had been up before and had told his grandfather where to go and exactly what to do.

Sometimes when we went up the mountain from Torver we used to eat our sandwiches in an old gunpowder hut just below the now disused Cove Quarries, and there were kegs of the stuff, I remember, lying about. Now the place is a climbing club hut and further up the mountain, in the quarry and looking across at the buttresses of Dow Crag, there's another climbing hut that some of us helped to build. I well remember dragging some of the long roof timbers up the fellside.

More indignities have been heaped upon the poor Old Man than upon any other Lake District mountain. Apart from the quarries and the derelict mine workings there are two roads up a considerable portion of the mountain—one to the Saddlestone quarries where the grey slate comes from (a tourist-littered high road in summer) and the other to Bursting Stone quarry where they win the sea-green Westmorland slate (although the mountain lies entirely in Lancashire). Then there's the tumble-down summit cairn, once a massive affair bigger than any other in Lakeland—the name 'Man' probably means 'a heap of stones' —but now an ugly ruin, with a survey-column close by. In places the mountain is hung with wire cables—there used to be many more of them—while some of the tarns have been tapped for water, and there was once a proposal to flood the Coppermines Valley for a hydro-electric scheme.

At one time there was a rifle-range on the Old Man's lower slopes and some years ago it was whispered they were looking for uranium near some of the abandoned workings. As I write they're talking about re-opening the copper mines. They've cut down the lovely larches in the wood near Church Beck, run huge pipe-lines down to the valley and planted sign-posts on the shoulders of the mountain, while motorists have bucketed across the flanks and over Walna Scar to the Duddon, and motor-cycles have been ridden to the very summit. But despite all this, and much more, the Old Man remains a fine mountain, and even the withdrawal of the railway service at his feet and the world's water speed records—and ultimate tragedy—achieved along his own lake have left him aloof, dignified and undisturbed.

Some of the finest tarns in Lakeland—Goats Water, Low Water, Levers Water and Blind Tarn—lie in his corries, the ravens still frequent his lonely crags, and harebells, eyebright and alpine mantle grow among the deserted shafts. You can see the tall chimneys of Calder Hall—and even Blackpool Tower —from the top but, on a winter's day, you can still feel a long way from the haunts of man up there, and far above the little things of life. For the Old Man will always remain for me a mountain of character.

Dow Crag

Dow Crag is the name of one of the most magnificent precipices in Lakeland and also the name of the mountain itself—one of the comparatively few instances in the district where the fell takes its name from its most prominent feature. Pillar, Dove Crag, Crinkle Crags and St. Sunday Crag are other examples.

It may be that I know Dow Crag better than any other mountain, for I've been climbing on it regularly for forty years, and must have visited it hundreds of times. I can't claim, however, to have been to the top hundreds of times, for rock climbers, I'm afraid, are too often content merely to reach the top of their climb and then scramble down an easy way, leaving the summit unvisited. But more times on Dow than on any other crag, I've carried on to the top of the ridge after completing a climb, looked out across Dunnerdale to the sunset and then continued over the Old Man and down through the lengthening shadows to the valley. So that Dow Crag has always been more to me than just a climbing ground, for in one way and another it has been associated with the best years in my life.

In the late 1920s nine of us formed a climbing club, calling ourselves, with youthful arrogance, the 'Coniston Tigers', and we lived every weekend in our own hut near Coniston Old Hall —perhaps the very first climbing hut in Lakeland. From here we used to venture forth on to Dow Crag, week after week, in all weathers, until we seemed to know every boulder on the way up and most of the holds on the precipice. We thought of it, selfishly, as 'our crag' and reckoned to know most of the people who went to climb there, but those glorious days of freedom are long since gone, and today, when I go up there, I hardly ever see anybody I know.

The first time I saw Dow Crag in close-up—I was a youngster scrambling alone down the western slopes of the Old Man—I thought it looked frightening. A black cloud was hanging above the precipice, which looked dark and forbidding, and the pool of Goatswater seemed like a bottomless pit. Then the happy voices and laughter of climbers came winging across the combe and I could see them, tiny specks, running down the zigzags on the screes towards the tarn, and my fears melted away. And today, although I've been on the crag on scores of dark days—in storm, mist, high winds, ice and snow—and have even seen terrible tragedy there, Dow Crag to me is not a depressing, forbidding place, but an exciting, friendly mountain packed full of happy, youthful memories.

We have always pronounced the name 'Doe', and, indeed, when I first went climbing there it was often spelled that way, but some of the old farmers and quarrymen still pronounce it 'Dow' which has a more rugged, craggy sound and is possibly more correct. The controversy has raged for years and I will not labour it here, other than to point out that there are several Dow Crags in Lakeland, and also to suggest that the fact that the adjoining peak is called Buck Pike is probably purely coincidental and hardly evidence enough for calling the crag Doe Crag and pronouncing it that way. So we'll stick to Dow and pronounce it how we like.

Dow Crag was associated with the very beginnings of climbing in Lakeland, Haskett Smith doing the first route there more than eighty years ago. Most of the pioneers—W. C. Slingsby, Geoffrey Hastings, the Hopkinson brothers, Owen Glynne Jones, the Abrahams, the Broadricks and the Woodhouses—did their early climbing on the crag and the names of many of the routes on Dow record much of the splendid history of the craft. The Fell and Rock Climbing Club of the English Lake District was born out of the early climbing expeditions to Dow Crag of men from the Barrow area and when I first went to the crag from the same district I felt I was treading hallowed ground. And I still do.

There are more than sixty different climbs on the crag, some of them among the most severe and exposed in Lakeland, but the crag is equally suitable for both novice and expert. The rock is splendidly weathered and normally extremely reliable although there have been fatalities due to holds coming away, and care is needed after the winter riving of the rock by the ice. The crag is 'clean', all the vegetation having been hacked off long ago, but not so scabbled as it used to be by nailed boots since the post-war fashion for boots with moulded rubber-soles. But on a wet, greasy day the ideal footwear for Dow, in my opinion, is still the clinker-nailed boot, which calls for precise footwork but is more reliable under these conditions, and to an old-fashioned climber like myself, rather more appropriate on a crag with so many traditions and memories.

It is difficult to catalogue so many memories in a short chapter but they include several meetings on the crag with men who shaped the course of British mountaineering. I remember, for instance, following up the crag a party which included the late Geoffrey Winthrop Young. He was climbing with his artificial leg, to which was attached a special device for rock work. George Bower, one of the Dow Crag pioneers who suggested the name for a new route some of us once put up on the crag, was, I think, in the party, and it was his father-in-law, George Basterfield, another leader on many first ascents on the crag, who had first introduced me to Dow. My first day's climbing on any major crag—under George's leadership—consisted of Woodhouses' Route and down Easter Gully, and then Arête, Chimney and Crack and down Great Gully—a good day, I think, for a novice, although some youngsters seem to start on 'severes' nowadays.

I've seen a man—the great Jim Birkett—climbing brilliantly on the crag wearing clogs circled with iron 'caulkers' and I once took a climber wearing pyjamas up one of the routes. I have fallen on the crag—but not very far—and seen another man fall nearly a hundred feet and escape with a slight knee injury. He rode home twenty-five miles on his motor-cycle and made me promise not to tell his mother of his fall. We have been wet through to the skin on Dow on many occasions and often climbed there when the precipice was sheathed in snow and ice. Often we have had the crag to ourselves, perhaps two of us, and there have been other days when almost every route has been festooned in ropes, and the place has looked like a circus. We used to see the peregrine there, but not now, although the ravens still circle the precipice. From one of the gullies I have looked down and seen two foxes, not one, crossing the screes far below, while we have fished for char in Goats Water, bathed there a score of times and even skated there. And there have been days when the spray from the waves on the tarn has been blown several hundreds of feet into the air and half-way up the crag and you had to fight every inch of the way even to get to the screes.

The shape of the crag has altered a little since I first knew it, some routes having been made more difficult through rock-falls and some perhaps easier. The cave at the foot of the crag has several times been rebuilt and there is now a stretcher and other first-aid equipment just below the rocks. In the old days the nearest stretcher was at Coniston and people unlucky enough to get injured were taken down the lower slopes on a horse-drawn cart. The spring near the foot of Intermediate Gully is one of the crag's most welcome provisions—it is always flowing even in the driest weather—but the bilberries have disappeared from the face of the crag and the hyacinths no longer grow on Hyacinth Terrace.

The summit of the crag is a superb eyrie but walkers can hardly taste the full flavour of the exposure of the precipice since most of the crag's steepness is concentrated in its lower half and the upper rocks ease off considerably. You only get the real feeling of Dow when you are perched half-way up the crag and looking out across the black pool of Goatswater at the craggy face of the Old Man, with the length of Coniston Water down below to the right and beyond that, in the distance, the waters of Morecambe Bay.

The sun leaves the face of the crag in the afternoon and on most days you finish your day's climbing in the shade. But the perfect finish to a day on Dow is to climb out to the top of the crag into the sunshine, look across Dunnerdale to the Scafells, and then slowly circle the combe to the Old Man and so, down through the bracken and the mellow evening to Coniston.

Perhaps I've missed out much of the portrait of the mountain, the old quarries on the way up, the prehistoric remains, the ancient route over Walna Scar, Blind Tarn, the long slopes into Dunnerdale and much more besides, but Dow Crag to me is the precipice—my favourite crag in the whole of Lakeland. Only a great lump of cliff to some people, but to a few of us a place that once meant more to us than anywhere else in the world. A place where, at just the right age, we not only found adventure, but also learned something about beauty and companionship that was to last us all our lives.

Wetherlam

One of the loveliest and most fascinating corners of Lakeland has always been for me the quiet wooded country between the Brathay and the Yewdale Fells. And the undoubted queen of this far-flung outpost of Lancashire is the great, rounded mass of Wetherlam—a hill, you might say, with much more to it than immediately meets the eye.

Wetherlam is not a very high mountain, but it has character, a fine, leonine shape as seen from Little Langdale, interesting associations with the long-forgotten past, a splendid view of the highest land in England from its rocky summit, and two counties at its feet. From my house near Kendal Wetherlam seems a bigger mountain than Coniston Old Man, and so it is—130 feet lower, certainly, but much more bulky and broad-shouldered; a rather shapeless, straggly sort of mountain, lacking a characteristic peak like Bowfell or Gable, and tending to merge with its neighbours, so that one is not always very clear where it starts and finishes. And often, especially when viewed from the south, Wetherlam seems to become merely the handmaiden to Coniston Old Man, the lesser background to the hoary giant.

But look at Wetherlam from the east or the north, and the mountain comes into its own, and, under the right conditions, can dominate the scene. Stand on the little heights around Tarn Hows, perhaps on a winter's afternoon with snow on the fells, and Wetherlam seems to fill the western sky. Or study the mountain from Little Langdale and note how it overshadows everything else.

Essentially, this is a fell to be studied from close at hand, and especially from Brathay or from Tilberthwaite where the past easily mingles with the present and the next hundred years will probably bring little change. It is so easy to people this area with ghosts—the old miners, Lanty Slee and his smuggling friends, the early quarrymen, the woodsmen and the charcoal burners— all gone so long ago but leaving behind their scars. And the remarkable thing about Wetherlam is that the mountain seems to have been able to absorb all this activity without damage, and, indeed, to have acquired distinction and character from its man-made shafts, caverns, tunnels and holes, its oddly-varied woodlands, hacked and hewn through the centuries, and even its overgrown spoil-heaps which, in season, can be rich with flowers. Walk on to the mountain from any direction and you will soon come upon evidence of the hand of man, but nobody could say that Wetherlam has been spoiled. Although men have been mining for copper or hewing for slate in these parts for hundreds of years nearly all the evidence of their toil is now either hidden in the tangled woods or merged into the knobbly fellside.

And it is the discovery of these things—the huge holes and tremendous shafts, for instance—that makes a visit to the

mountain particularly worthwhile. Many times, on days unsuit-
able for the tops or the crags, we've gone exploring these places,
and there are few better ways of filling in a December day, or
perhaps a spring afternoon when wind and rain have driven you
down from the heights.

There are some places on the mountain where you can walk
right into the fell and emerge into the open air some distance
away, and for the young and active—and especially those with
some climbing experience—all sorts of interesting expeditions
can be devised. More than once we've taken a rope into the
quarries above Little Langdale Tarn and found plenty of good
fun and exercise, both below and above ground level. Some of
these holes are among the biggest in Lakeland, and the casual
visitor should be warned that most of the shafts are dangerous
and should be boarded up. There must have been tragedies in
these dark pits which, for the most part, do not lend themselves
to proper potholing exploration since they are crumbling and
half-filled with water and rubbish. Half-hearted attempts seem
to have been made to fence them off from time to time, but little
real good achieved. The shafts can easily be avoided during
daytime, but can be a menace at night or in mist, and could
easily trap a sheep or a dog. It is remarkable that we never seem
to hear of terrible tragedies in these desperate places nowadays
and I think a good case could be made out for sealing up the
worst of the shafts in the Wetherlam and Coniston Old Man
area. It would not be an impossible task for parties of properly
organized volunteers—National Park wardens perhaps—to
board them over or block up the openings in some way.

But an adventurous youngster, with the necessary skill, can
get a lot of fun in the tunnels and also in the quarry holes and
caves. Some of these holes—big enough to hide a cathedral, or,
at least, a big church—are tremendously impressive, especially
when it is realized that they were hacked out for the most part
by men hanging from the roof in chains, or blasted by old-
fashioned and dangerous methods. There are huge holes open
to the sky, caverns in the fellside with great vaulted ceilings,
gigantic columns of rock, massive archways, underground lakes
and other exciting things—mostly hidden in the woods. Some
of the holes and caverns are not seen until you are almost at their
edge or entrance, and are all the more impressive for being so
unexpected. Inside, everything is deathly quiet, but sometimes
you can hear a distant drip of water echoing through the
caverns like a gong.

And sometimes an owl will come winging through the dark woods above the Brathway and around Tilberthwaite, which are among the most interesting in southern Lakeland because of the many varieties of trees. Often I've spent a pleasant winter's afternoon trying to identify all the trees in their leafless state as I wandered and scrambled about the holes and tunnels. In one of the disused quarries is one of the caves where the notorious Lanty Slee made his whisky and you can still see where he had his still and his tiny cellar. Later he smuggled the stuff over the passes or sold it locally—at 10s. a gallon. I knew Lanty's son and last spoke to him soon after he had celebrated his 100th birthday when he told me his father's brew was the best and most potent whisky ever to come out of Lakeland.

Some of the quarries in the area are still in operation, and particularly busy these days satisfying the new demand for great slabs of green stone for the outside cladding of buildings. The mines that ring Wetherlam are old copper mines, and, if you know where to look among the bushes of stunted juniper, you can still spot the copper ore in the rock. They mined at Red Dell, at Paddy End, at Church Beck, above Tilberthwaite on Birk Fell, high up on the northern front of Wetherlam, in Greenburn, and in several other places, and everywhere they left their shafts and levels.

There are said to be wild goats on Wetherlam but although I've known the mountain all my life, I've never seen any of them. Several years ago they were said to graze among the high rocks during the summer and come down towards the hamlets in the winter time. They make better cragsmen than sheep and were probably originally introduced to keep the sheep away from the cliffs, for sheep and goats rarely get on well together. At one time the quarrymen of Tilberthwaite and Little Langdale used to gather at Easter for an annual goat hunt, but I don't think that much slaughter was done, for the goats would probably be more agile than the dalesmen.

The splendid ravine of Tilberthwaite bites deeply into the eastern slopes of Wetherlam. Years ago it was laddered quite a long way up but on my last visit the ladders only reached its foot. Storms and years of neglect washed away the old timbers and I was glad they'd not been replaced. Although ladders and bridges might make these sort of places accessible to people who otherwise would not be able to penetrate there, I've never liked them and have always considered this sort of expenditure both wasteful and selfish. Fortunately nobody has yet suggested

laddering Piers Gill on the side of Lingmell, a much more
spectacular ravine, and I hope they never will.

Just below the summit of Wetherlam on the southern side
there is a small crag, Hen Tor, which makes a prominent
feature during the winter snows but it is hardly noticed in
summer. There is a summer climb up the side of the crag and a
snow climb up the gully in winter. A little to the west of the
summit is a tiny rocky pool and, about half a mile away, a
secondary summit, Black Sails, which is sometime ascended in
mistake for the real top. The south ridge of the mountain is
named Lad Stones on the maps but the quarrymen only know it
as 'La'al Gladstone'. Possibly the early mapmakers misheard
the local name, as they so often did in the Lakeland fells.

Undoubtedly there's much more to Wetherlam than there is
to many much bigger Lakeland hills, and I will always remember
the mountain with affection for it belongs to my youth. As
youngsters we must have enjoyed every sort of adventure up
there, sometimes getting lost or getting knocks and minor
injuries, but we kept going back, for it seemed a different sort
of mountain and the more we explored it, the friendlier it
became. And it still seems a friendly mountain today.

Swirl How

Swirl How—suggesting fresh air, remoteness and winter blizzards—is a fine, brave name for a mountain. And this picture is
often not far from the truth, for Swirl How is a shy, rather lonely
fell, not nearly so often visited as its neighbours, exposed to
the cold winds from the north-east, and generally displaying a
mood of craggy defiance.

The mountain faces Westmorland down the long, lonely
trough of Greenburn and peers over Wrynose to Cumberland
and the Scafells but is, of course, in Lancashire. It is, in fact,
the second highest mountain in the county—topped by Coniston
Old Man by only three feet—but lies only a mile or so inside the
boundary that also embraces so many industrial towns and cities.
From many angles it is a fine, wedge-shaped peak, marked on all
maps, but surprisingly ignored by the guide-books. Wainwright
mentions it, of course, but looking through more than a dozen
popular guide-books I find the mountain only mentioned twice
and then very briefly. Indeed, a list of the sixty principal mountains of Lakeland misses out Swirl How altogether.

And yet this shy peak, so often hidden by its satellites, could be regarded in some ways as the 'queen' of the Coniston Fells. From a handsome summit it radiates swinging ridges to the four points of the compass while its streams flow into all three counties, whereas Coniston Old Man, the accepted 'king' of the Coniston Fells, with its streams descending only on the Lancashire side, is really no more than the culminating point of one of its ridges. And then Swirl How, unlike the Old Man, is only disfigured by the hand of man on its lower slopes and is spared the indignity of slated tracks and roads, aerial cable-ways, huts and spoil-heaps. The Old Man, of course, retains his dignity while remaining the popular mountain, but the scarred veteran really only lords it over the county palatine by the height of a load of rubble, while the graceful peak of Swirl How remains unsung. Of the two fells the Old Man, of course, has much the stronger character, but it is nice to know that two miles further north you can get away from the summer crowds and tread a mountain, only fractionally lower, but more or less devoid of orange-peel and sandwich wrappings.

For me, Swirl How—like Coniston Old Man—is very much a mountain of boyhood memories and its rocky ridges of Prison Band and Great How Crags are places which, nearly forty years ago, we knew as well as our roads at home. We were up there in all weathers and at all seasons of the year, sometimes coming up Greenburn from Little Langdale and kicking steps in the snow to the top of the hause and so up Prison Band to the summit. Or we would come from Coniston and through the Coppermines Valley on a hot summer's afternoon or work along the ridge from the Old Man in autumn or spring to round off a climbing day on Dow Crag. And often the mountain would be the half-way stage in a round of the Coniston tops which would include Wetherlam, the two Carrs, Grey Friar, besides the Old Man, Brim Fell, and perhaps Dow Crag and Buck Pike—almost as fine a mountain round, taken in either direction, as you will get anywhere in Lakeland.

I have noted that the hand of man is not apparent on Swirl How, for neither the disused copper works in Greenburn nor the mine shafts and spoil-heaps on the other side of the mountain, below Levers Water, obtrude, and could, indeed, be associated with other fells. While the ugly wreckage of an aircraft high up above Greenburn is really an incident on the side of Great Carrs, its outlier, and not on Swirl How itself.

Of course, the old miners knew Swirl How well even if the old guide-book writers missed it out. They were always known as 'the old men' and, indeed, the work was so exacting that they were often, in fact, old men by middle age. Quite close to Levers Water which was used as a reservoir by the Paddy End and Coniston copper mines, is the notorious Simon's Nick—a vertical slice out of a wall of rock with a deep shaft below. This place is said to have been worked by a certain Simon Puchberger who struck a rich vein of copper ore and told his workmates he had been guided there by the fairies—or, as some said, by the Devil. But his working was robbed time and again until one day Simon, careless with his gunpowder work, either deliberately or by accident, blew himself up. They say the place is still haunted by his ghost.

This is only one of several old mine-shafts scattered about the lower slopes of the mountain that could be dangerous. Animals have died miserable deaths in these dark holes from time to time and maybe human beings have perished there, so there is much to be said for the shafts being sealed up or at least properly fenced in. They say that mining might have been going on in the Coniston Fells for two thousand years; some claim the Romans mined there but this has never been proved. In the early nineteenth century hundreds of men and boys worked in these mines but the decline began about ninety years ago and they were later abandoned. I remember as a boy poking about in the spoil heaps looking for crystals of copper or pyrites and I've always felt a fascination for old workings like these. At one time, I believe, copper in its malleable state was found underneath Swirl How and above Levers Water—the only place they say, where this has been found in Britain. Iron, too, has been found in the area.

Levers Water may have been spoiled to some extent by its dam but this is not very obtrusive and the basin is still a lovely spot on a summer's evening. Trout live in the tarn and are sometimes caught, but I've never seen anybody fishing there. The two other tarns that lie on the flanks of Swirl How—Greenburn and Seathwaite—are also reservoirs, the latter supplying Barrow Corporation. But you can turn your back to the dam at Seathwaite and still be moved by the fine shapes of Swirl How and Grey Friar, especially when they are under snow.

One particularly interesting walk is to climb Swirl How from Coniston, following Church Beck to the copper mines and then continuing past Levers Water to Swirl Hause, up Prison Band to the summit, down over Great How Crags to the col near Brim Fell, descending Cove Beck to Simon's Nick and so back to

Coniston again. With potholing tackle and some experience many of the old shafts and caves may be explored but if you lack either or both, they should merely be studied from above. The old ruins and the watercourses are also worth looking at, and with a little imagination you should be able to get an impression of what the area must have looked like a hundred or more years ago.

Just south of the track before Simon's Nick and Levers Water are reached you can branch off to explore Boulder Valley, a miniature climbing ground where problems of every kind may be found on a dozen or so huge boulders. The biggest of them is the Pudding Stone, one of the largest boulders in Lakeland, with a dozen climbing routes to the top, some of them very hard indeed. I once fell off one of them as a lad and recommend a rope for the harder ones. There are also the Inaccessible Boulder, which is rather easier than it sounds, and the Beck Stone where you risk a soaking if you fall off.

On a summer Sunday with the top of the Old Man crowded with people you can walk along the ridge, passing Brim Fell on the way, and perhaps never meet a soul. And once on Swirl How it is no great strain to continue on to Carrs or to swing across to the lonely and beautifully-named peak of Grey Friar. From the summit of Swirl How you can look northwards to Skiddaw, south to Walney Island, westwards to the Isle of Man and eastwards to the Pennines. Perhaps the view of the Scafells to the north-west is the best, but the sight of the sun setting over the Isle of Man can also be a wonderful experience. The view from Swirl How is finer than the one you get from the Old Man and you have a good chance of enjoying it alone. So I hope that Swirl How will continue to be ignored by the guide-book writers, remaining the preserve of those who take the trouble to seek it out to enjoy the unsung attractions of one of the best things in Lancashire.

2

MOUNTAINS FOR ADVENTURE

(The Wasdale Hills)

Scafell

THE sprawling switchback of the Scafell range is Nature's proudest landmark between Snowdon and the Scottish Highlands, and its finest single feature is the tremendous north-facing precipice that adorns the peak lying nearest to the sea. Scafell Crag is the name of the 600-feet-high rock wall—the biggest cliff in England—and we call the peak itself Scafell.

Ask the average Lakeland lover, resident or visitor, to draw, as roughly as he likes, the shape of Scafell and he'll probably fail. He might be able to give you the rounded dome of Gable, the pointed peak of Bowfell, the turrets of the Langdale Pikes or even the broad rooftree of Scafell Pike, but he can't for the life of him draw Scafell. And he may not even be able to identify it from a distance. For Scafell is, in many ways, a mountain without a shape, and its summit, overshadowed or hidden by the neighbouring Pike, seems unimportant. What matters is its northern face, the great crag and its outliers, so that to me Scafell, above all other mountains in Lakeland, is the climbers' mountain.

Long years ago, before the map-makers discovered the Lakeland mountains, the dalesmen knew the mountain range as Scafell—or probably Scaw Fell in those days—and later gave the name to the western peak which perhaps seemed the highest, and certainly the most impressive, summit in the range. The adjoining summit became 'the pikes near Scaw Fell'—the pikes being the minarets of Pikes Crag—and today we know this peak as Scafell Pike—the highest mountain in England. And even the latest issue of the Ordnance Survey names this mountain—in small type—Scafell *Pikes*, reserving its biggest print for Scafell. So that Scafell Pike is the highest mountain in England—and, indeed, even a separate mountain—almost incidentally. The real mountain, you could say, is Scafell. In Scotland the whole range, including Broad Crag, Ill Crag, and Great End, would be one mountain—another An Teallach or Ben Eighe—and the ascent of all five tops would count as one 'Munro'. In England, with fewer mountains to claim, we have to count them all and this little portrait is merely of the western peak.

It is easy to justify Scafell as the climbers' mountain. People don't walk up there in droves, as they do up the Pike or Gable or Helvellyn, and, indeed, the summit is only easily attainable from the west. From other directions the top must be reached by scrambling and the direct route from Scafell Pike involves the ascent of a moderate rock-climb—the only instance in England where the ordinary tourist, crossing from one mountain to the next, must find another way. So that the summit has a slight air of invulnerability, and you are less likely than on the more popular summits to meet people up there in high-heeled shoes or city wear. Most people encountered on the top know where they are and what they are doing, and there is still, thank God, no broad, cairned highway to the summit with bottles and tins under every stony heap.

In common with most Lake District mountains of character Scafell presents two completely contrasting faces to an admiring world—broad, featureless slopes dipping westwards and southerly towards Wasdale and Eskdale and, to north and east, the great wall of shadowed crags that, under certain conditions, can make the mountain appear an awesome, even frightening, place. To me, therefore, Scafell is hardly a friendly, shapely mountain like Bowfell or a beautiful peak like Gable, but rather the remarkable combination of an almost commonplace hump and the most savage barrier of naked rock and scree in England. But although its sunless sides are too ferocious to be beautiful in the limited sense of the word these cathedral-like buttresses and pinnacles have a majesty and grandeur which the climber can find quite irresistible. Scafell Crag and the East Buttress, on the other side of Mickledore, together present Nature's biggest challenge to muscle, nerve and skill in the district for, as often as not, height must be won on these stern, uncompromising walls when they are hung in mists, streaming with water or merely dark and cold. You may climb in the sunshine on warm, friendly rocks on Pikes Crag just across the wilderness of Hollow Stones, but rarely on Scafell.

The great crags of Scafell have many famous associations for the climber. There are the stories of Owen Glynne Jones crawling in his stockinged feet up the Pinnacle more than sixty years ago, Fred Botterill's remarkable lead up his great slab at the beginning of the century, the tragedy high up on the Pinnacle Face in the same year, the ascent of Central Buttress—easily the hardest climb in Britain at the time—by Herford and Sansom in 1914, and the determined assaults on the overhanging walls of the East Buttress which were to come later. These and many other remarkable and, in a few cases, tragic exploits have given the crags their traditions and atmosphere so that the present-day climber working his way up the face knows he is stepping where the very greatest men in his craft have gone before him. For all of us who go to Scafell to climb, these rocks are hallowed ground.

Even Broad Stand, the simple little climb that stands in the way of the ordinary tourist wishing to pass from Scafell Pike to Scafell, has its history for it may well be that the poet Coleridge made its first descent, which would make this rather unlikely-sounding candidate almost the first rock-climber. Coleridge went up the mountain from Wasdale and down into Eskdale in 1802 and his description of the descent, written partly for the Wordsworths, ties up exactly with the situation and shape (including the 'chasm' at the bottom) of Broad Stand. Local dalesmen probably made the first ascent—at least nine years before Pillar Rock was first climbed in 1826.

I have many happy memories of Scafell—summer days of achievement on the classic rock-climbs, wintry days in Deep Gill, wild, wet and windy days searching for the summit, perfect sunny evenings running down the pleasant slopes of Green How, and one day when, having got my dog up the West Wall Traverse I failed, because of ice, to get him down Broad Stand.

One of my oldest memories is of a night spent on the summit. Two of us—youngsters in our teens—left a camp in Eskdale and trudged up the dreary slopes above Burnmoor to reach the top just before night closed in. But before darkness came we had the wonderfully rewarding experience of looking down on a Lakeland covered in cotton-wool clouds with only the topmost peaks of Gable and the rest sticking up above the billowing whiteness. It was a cold night and we shivered, without tent or sleeping

Scafell and Scafell Pike
Scafell Crag (overleaf)

bags, for hours but eventually the dawn came up over Langdale and soon the summit rocks were flooded in the brightest sunlight.

There may be better viewpoints in Lakeland than the summit of Scafell but I have never seen so remarkable a view as the one we enjoyed about six o'clock that perfect morning nearly forty years ago. From the summit we could see the Lowland peaks of Scotland with a clarity I have never known since and across the blue, dancing waters of the Irish Sea we could see Ireland, probably Slieve Donard in County Down, perfectly plainly, while the Isle of Man looked close enough to be within swimming range. We moved across the summit for perhaps a hundred yards so that we could look to the south and there on the farthest horizon, beyond the very end of the sea, we could pick out the tops of distant mountains, only just discernible in the clear morning air. The mountains of Snowdonia, probably the Glyders, we decided, and having made many inquiries since into the possibility of so distant a view I've found no reason to change our opinion. So that, from the summit of Scafell, under absolutely perfect conditions, it may be possible to see—but not from exactly the same place—England, Scotland, Ireland and Wales.

In many ways Scafell is a remarkable mountain, but not only because of its grandeur, its great crags, its comparative impregnability, and its wonderful views. Just below the summit to the east of the main ridge is a lonely, hanging valley and, almost hidden among the rocks, is Fox Tarn—the second highest tarn in Lakeland. It is also easily the smallest tarn to possess a name, and is one of the rather lesser-known treasures of Scafell—our most exciting mountain.

Scafell Pike

The discovery of the Lake District, it has been written, could be said to have been completed when William Wordsworth climbed to the top of Scafell Pike on 7th October 1818. Not many tourists before him had thought it worth while scrambling to the highest point in England and, indeed, it is not clear whether anybody then realized that there was nothing any higher. For the mountain was not even properly named in those days, although a few years later it was said that the shepherds knew it as 'the Pikes near Scafell'.

In the intervening century and a half since Wordsworth's

3

Eagle's Nest Arête on Great Gable
(*Napes Needle is low on the right*)
Great Gable and Kirk Fell from High Crag (facing)

visit the shape of Scafell Pike hasn't altered very much, apart from the addition of its huge, ugly cairn and the Ordnance Survey triangulation column, but the mountain has become a Mecca for thousands of weary pilgrims each year, just because it happens to be higher than anywhere else. The views are as good, if not better, from some other Lakeland mountains, but while hardly anybody bothers to go to the top of Broad Crag or Ill Crag, less than half a mile away and nearly as high, the rocky track to the Pike becomes almost a crowded highway on summer weekends. Nearly every scrap of vegetation has been kicked and trodden off the top—they say the dwarf willow used to grow up there, but I've never found it—and the tracks have been scratched into white thoroughfares across the grey wilderness of rocks. If you keep to the tracks you can't easily get lost on the top of the Pike, even in mist. Litter abounds up there on the worst days, sometimes disgustingly blowing about in the breeze, and gangs of voluntary wardens, Outward Bound students and Boy Scouts have to go up regularly to do other people's scavenging. So the summit is not really an especially attractive place and even less so when it's crowded.

Many indignities have been perpetrated on top. Beacon and bonfire lightings, flag flyings, tablet unveilings and services and meetings of many kinds may be excused, but the dragging to the summit and dumping there of an old iron bedstead was deplorable.

Perhaps the strange thing about Scafell Pike is that although thousands go up there every year and the tracks across its top are the easiest to follow in the district, the mountain is, in some ways, almost a secret place. It is hidden from many parts of Lakeland by its bulky neighbours and on some of the ascents the summit is masked for most of the way. Its shape is not nearly as recognizable as those of several much lower Lakeland summits and the peak is frequently seen more as a wrinkle on a ridge than the highest point in the country. The cairn on its dome-shaped summit is very prominent but it is the long ridge of the Scafells as a whole, the most rugged mountain mass in England, that is memorable, and not the slight protuberance of the Pike itself.

While people are going up and down its tracks almost every day of the year, very few bother really to explore the mountain, especially the wild eastern slopes. So it cannot be said that Scafell Pike is well known in the way that Bowfell or Great Gable are, for almost all the visitors stick to the main highways.

The reason for this is that the mountain—few people refer to the Pike as a fell—is quite a long walk from any centre and attracts every type of walker, including the least experienced, because of its pre-eminence as a height rather than for its splendours. And many of these visitors find the going long enough and tough enough on the ordinary paths without bothering to go exploring.

But this is the roughest and rockiest country in England as well as the highest. The mountain is girdled with crags on all sides, its summit heaped with boulders, and its slopes strewn with screes so that although all the tourist ascents are easy they are all long and slow. You can't trip up and down Scafell Pike anything like as quickly as you can Helvellyn.

The real rewards of the Pike are away from the tourist routes and the litter. How many of the thousands who haul themselves to the top, for instance, know Broad Crag Tarn, about a quarter of a mile south-west of the summit, but some distance away from the usual track? This is the highest tarn in Lakeland, being 2,746 feet above sea-level—an impressive little pool lying in a basin of solid rock, not far from the ridge of Mickledore and the dark overhangs of East Buttress on Scafell. The smallest tarn in Lakeland, and the second highest, is Fox Tarn or Foxes Tarn, just across the rocky scramble out of Eskdale to the Mickledore gap.

And how many Scafell visitors know the great cliff of Dow Crag, one of many similarly named precipices in Lakeland, that lies low down on the Eskdale side of the summit? Climbers know the crag, one of the steepest in Lakeland, as Esk Buttress. Not many of the people who walk up and down the mountain by the tourist paths bother to walk across to the fine pinnacle of Pulpit Rock overlooking Hollow Stones—the finest viewpoint for Scafell Crag, which is the most remarkable cliff in England. And how many reach the summit by way of the upper Esk and the steep, rocky defile of Little Narrowcove—Little 'Arra, to the dalesfolk? I once went this way on a bright October morning, walking nor' nor' west from Cockley Beck, up Moasdale and over all the little craggy bumps between the Lingcove and the Esk. Then straight up to the cove and one of the most wonderful camping sites in Lakeland, perched just underneath the highest crags in England. This way you get the full flavour of the mountain—full in view as a craggy, sprawling mass for miles and then two thousand feet of height to be won within a mile of the Esk.

You can wander about these craggy slopes on the Eskdale side when the popular routes are crowded and hardly see a soul all day. Once during a climbing expedition to Esk Buttress we watched shepherds from Brotherilkeld Farm winkling out fox cubs from a borran right underneath the crag. And some of my best memories of Scafell Pike are of climbing in late evening sunshine up the walls and chimneys of Pikes Crag when the other cliffs were shadowed and quiet and we seemed to have the mountain to ourselves.

Scafell Pike could be called the king of English mountains but you've got to get to know him to appreciate this. There's more to learn about this range than any other mountain group in the country and its potential dangers for the inexperienced tourist are greater than anywhere else in Lakeland. The Scafells form the only mountain ridge that cannot be traversed by the ordinary walker who, to avoid the rock-climb of Broad Stand, has to make a wide detour to go from the Pike to Scafell. While immediately below the tourist path of the Corridor Route there is the tremendous ravine of Piers Gill which can be a death trap for the unwary and is only negotiable by climbers during periods of exceptionally dry weather. And on the other side of the mountain, overlooking the Upper Esk, is the wildest and roughest country in Lakeland. But the youngsters in low shoes who set off each summer weekend to climb to the highest point in England don't know these things and so we have the accidents and the mountain searches. Every year inexperienced people go up from Borrowdale by the Corridor Route, from Langdale by way of Esk Hause, or from Wasdale by Hollow Stones in poor equipment or in bad weather and get back exhausted and often fed up with mountains. And some have died because they underestimated the size of the mountain or its savagery in storm or in winter-time. Many ill-led school parties have been lucky to get down unscathed. These tourist paths will not teach the visitor a great deal about this great sprawling mountain, and off these well-trodden ways Scafell Pike is hardly a place for the tourist. To get to know the real Scafell Pike you should have the necessary mountain experience to explore the mountain in all weathers and at all seasons.

The name 'Scawfell Pike' or 'Scawfell' has crept into some guides, maps and hotel names because of the pronunciation. The accent, of course, should be on the first syllable as in nearly all Lakeland place names—Keswick, Penrith, Bowness, Loughrigg and so on—but the derivation, I'm told, is 'sca' or 'scar', a Norse word meaning steep or sheer, the word 'scaw' being meaningless. The shepherd says 'Scarf'l' or something like it but if you pronounce the name of the highest mountain in England as '*Scawf*'l Pike'—although writing it Scafell—you won't be far wrong.

Great Gable

Everybody knows Great Gable, either by sight or by name. The finest mountain in England, many folk say—fine both to look at and to look from; the Queen of the Lakeland fells. To most people it is a shapely triangle, nicely centred between Kirkfell—or Yewbarrow—on the left, and Lingmell leading up to Scafell Pike on the right. This is the popular view of the mountain from the shore of Wastwater, the view that the Lake District Planning Board uses as the emblem for the National Park, and one of the most photographed views in the district.

In this scene Gable appears graceful and serene, the natural centre-piece of the finest ring of fells in this country, and the dark surface of Wastwater sets off a picture of calm majesty. Sometimes we see the shadows of the clouds chasing across the bare, rocky mountainside and now and again there is a wisp of white or grey caught on the pointed summit. As we draw nearer to the finest valley head in England we can see the thin scratch of the track over the Sty zigzagging up the fellside and, if the day is clear enough and we know where to look, we can pick out the Needle, high up among the clustered Napes ridges.

But this view is not necessarily the most typical of this fine mountain, for Gable is not always an elegant and smiling fell and from some directions may even appear a savage, almost ugly lump. To the motorist she may show herself as a graceful cone but to the walker and climber she can be a great rounded hump thrusting into the sky, almost impregnably ringed with crags. From the Helvellyn range, for instance, Gable looks not unlike Suilven in the Northern Highlands—a broad dome with steep crags at either end—and this less elegant but more impressive view more closely suggests the true character of the mountain. For Great Gable, however friendly she may appear from the patchwork fields in Wasdale Head, is not merely a picture-postcard mountain, but a mountain of character, independent, savagely moody at times, challenging, steep, almost completely bare of vegetation and always inspiring.

Gable must contain a higher percentage of crag and scree than almost any other mountain in Lakeland and there is perhaps no other mountain in the National Park more uniformly steep on all sides. With crags almost all the way round and no grassy run-off to speak of, it is, more than any other of our fells, a rock mountain. And the screes that almost encircle the mountain tell their story of the great crags that must have girdled the summit tens of thousands of years ago.

The mountain has no hidden combes nor hanging valleys nor wooded ravines but is more or less straight up and down all the way round, and this steepness gives the walker or climber a feeling of airiness that he may not experience on other, even higher, Lakeland fells. From the topmost block on the Needle, for instance, you can almost imagine yourself suspended in space and you feel you could almost throw a stone down to Wasdale Head or, at least, to the foot of the mountain. The fells around the lake, including the dark rampart of The Screes look curiously flattened from this airy perch, while the hotel, the farms and the tiny church amid the yew trees appear rather like wooden models stuck on a cardboard base of painted fields. Away in the distance, beyond the lake and the coastal plains, is the sea, perhaps glittering in the sunlight, while around you the shattered ridges soar towards the summit. Only one landmark seems to retain its stature and majesty—the great, black precipice of Scafell Crag hanging over the shoulder of Lingmell. The walker gets a similar view—although not quite so striking—from the cairn on Westmorland Crag, just below the summit on the 'popular' side—a view that has sometimes been described as the best in the country.

Everybody who is interested knows the story of how Napes Needle was first climbed by the great W. P. Haskett Smith in 1886 and how Owen Glynne Jones was stirred to begin his Lakeland climbing by the sight of a photograph of the Needle in a shop in the Strand. Many very much harder climbs than the Needle have since been made on Gable but this shapely spire, perhaps unnoticed by some walkers, is still the most famous bit of rock in England and is climbed by hundreds of people every year. People have lit fires on the top block, shaved and breakfasted there, or stood on their heads and once, many years ago, I was involved in a project which, perhaps fortunately, never matured, to camp out for an hour or two on the top in a bivouac tent. A few yards away from the Needle is the steep, impressive ridge of Eagle's Nest Arête, first climbed on a cold April morning in 1892 by G. A. Solly and three companions—one of the most daring leads of the nineteenth century and the hardest climb in the country up to that time. And nearer to the top of the Sty are the climbs, first pioneered by O. G. Jones, on Kern Knotts—a steep little crag of considerable character but rather too close to the track for those of us who prefer to climb un- watched and out of camera range.

But the striking feature of the mountain for the climber are the soaring Napes Ridges—the shattered ribs of sound rock that give him a little of the exhilaration of swarming up the Swiss aiguilles with fresh air all around and steep drops on either side. You don't often get this feeling on Lakeland rock, even on very much harder routes, and this, for me, helps to give Gable something of a holiday atmosphere. We often went to Wasdale for our holidays as youngsters, for, unlike Coniston and Langdale, it was too far away to go by bicycle on an ordinary weekend.

On a wall in my study hangs a photograph of the Needle, taken on an all-night winter walk from Coniston when we were youngsters. It was a time exposure shot about 4 a.m. and shows the Needle, lit by the moon and sheathed in ice. For years it was my most treasured picture, and it still reminds me of happy, care-free days when nothing really mattered except the hills.

Gable Crag on the less-visited side of the mountain is a fine, north-facing precipice which can be a delightful haven of solitude when the more popular climbs are too crowded for enjoyment. It is a curiously neglected crag, containing several old-fashioned but worthwhile routes, including Smugglers Chimney, where I once remember having an awkward five minutes when a slim book carried in a breast-pocket com- pletely jammed me in the narrow cleft. Some distance up the crag are the remains of what might have been a stone hut and tradition has it that 'Moses', a quarryman turned whisky- distiller and smuggler, used this as a hideout. Another theory is that it might have been used as a store for wad or plumbago stolen from the mine near Seathwaite. Moses' Trod is the well- graded track that passes along the 'back' of Gable towards the top of Honister, and Moses' Finger, the prominent boulder at the top of the steep grass slope of Gavel Neese.

But Gable is not only a climbers' playground. Its summit, for ordinary walkers, is one of the most popular in Lakeland although the multiplicity of cairns is quite unnecessary and has led more than one walker down to Windy Gap when he was looking for Beck Head. A bronze plaque mounted among the highest rocks indicates the war memorial of the Fell and Rock Climbing Club, the actual memorial being the surrounding central summits of Lakeland, and a simple service is held there, no matter what the weather, every November. You will often find a pool of rain-water caught in these summit rocks even in time of drought, a point worth remembering for Gable can be a very dry, stony mountain. There is, too, not far from Kern Knotts, a tiny spring that I have never known to fail in more than forty years.

The stony track over the Sty that winds across the face of Gable is a romantic route, the only direct connection between Borrowdale and Wasdale and a route that has little altered in the last few hundred years. On many occasions a road has been threatened across this lonely pass, but such an 'improvement' will surely never come about, for the opposition is much too strong. The two dale heads would be flooded with motor traffic if this sort of thing was ever tackled and the tranquillity of the central fells lost for ever.

For some, Gable is a tragic mountain, and if you visit the tiny church among the yews you will see the climbers' graves in the churchyard. Two or three, but not all, were killed on Gable but all knew the mountain well and they lie there because they loved the hills. So that Gable is not always the friendly mountain you see from the lake shore; it is a challenge and an inspiration and it can also be a warning.

But Great Gable is the favourite Lakeland mountain for many people and for me will always be my holiday mountain. It is so easy to recall many, many happy days as a youth, climbing its airy ridges, racing down its dusty screes, walking over the mountain by moonlight, bathing and skating at Styhead Tarn, searching for garnets in the boulders on the Wasdale side and striding down through the bracken after a strenuous day on warm, sunlit rocks for tea and scones in a cool, shadowed room.

Kirk Fell

The bulky, rather shapeless mass of Kirk Fell, next door neighbour to Great Gable, must be one of the most neglected mountains in Lakeland. Although it lies in the very centre of the most celebrated mountain group in England it is still comparatively untracked and relatively few people bother to scramble to its summit. Or rather, summits, for there are two of them—half a mile apart and one about fifty feet higher than the other. If you drive your car to Wasdale Head, the traditional centre for mountaineering in this country, step out at the end of the lane, and carry on straight ahead on foot, you are starting on the ascent of Kirk Fell, for the mountain overshadows the hamlet. But you hardly ever see anybody doing this.

When we first used to go to Wasdale Head towards the end of the 1920s we considered that the grass tongue of Kirk Fell leading down to the inn was the steepest grass in Lakeland and this seemed good enough reason for not going up that way. No doubt there are any number of even steeper grass slopes in the district, but this one has always seemed sufficiently tilted to deter the average, casual walker, so that nearly all the tourist traffic goes past the foot of poor, lonely Kirk Fell or round his flank towards Black Sail.

No mountain could be more perfectly situated for popularity than this great hump of a fell that always looks to me like a magnificent peak from which the top has dropped away. Wasdale Head at its very foot, the much-used passes of Sty Head and Black Sail on its flanks, and shapely Great Gable just a short distance away across the col of Beck Head. But ninety-nine people out of a hundred hurry on past it, while some folk admire it from afar, believing they are looking at Gable, for the Queen of the Lakeland Fells is obscured by the more humble Kirk Fell from some directions.

Few of the guide-books bother to mention Kirk Fell and an old one of mine dated 1916, dismisses it briefly with: "No track and very steep and slippery. A long grind." Nothing about the mountain nor the quality of the views from the top; a mountain, apparently, hardly worth bothering with. There even seems some doubt about how its name should be spelled, but the Ordnance Survey make it two words so I'll stick to this form instead of the rather more frequently used Kirkfell.

I suppose the principal reason for the neglect of this fine, broad-shouldered lump of mountain is that it is so close to even better things—next door to Gable, immediately facing Scafell and the Pikes, the highest land in England, and only separated by Black Sail Pass from Pillar and its great Rock. Small wonder, perhaps, that so many people walk round it on their way to what they believe to be even more delectable heights. And when, to the magnificence of its immediate neighbours, are added the steepness of its rather dull slopes, its comparative lack of feature when seen from Wasdale and its apparent absence of summit—it is really an uplifted plateau—its neglect by the unenterprising can be understood.

But Kirk Fell is deserving of better treatment than this. It may be a dull hump of a mountain from some sides, and may not have the panache of Gable nor the superiority of Scafell, but it is still a worthy mountain—not so high as Gable but nearly twice its bulk, its broad top one of the most wonderful viewpoints in Lakeland, and its little summit tarns providing the perfect upland scene on a warm, summer's day. There are a few higher tarns than these in Lakeland, but Kirk Fell is among a tiny handful of mountains that can boast tarns so near their summits. These two lie not far short of the 2,500-feet contour and are contained in the hollow between the two summits. They sparkle in the summer sunshine among the mountain grasses and outcrops of pink-grey rock, and if you go up there even on August Monday you will probably be alone with the mountain birds. On the right day the air can be filled with the song of skylarks and meadow pipits and you can dream away a lazy afternoon, sitting in the sunshine and admiring the view.

From the tops or the tarns you look out across the Lingmell Beck at the whole, long line of the Scafell range, notched against the sky, or you can admire the unusual 'side' view of Gable, or the switchback of the Buttermere fells, or the sweep of Pillar from Looking Stead. You can reach this perfect viewpoint from the top of Styhead—if you don't like the steep Wasdale slope—by way of the climbers' track underneath the Napes ridges, or round the 'back' of Gable by Aaron Slack or by scrambling up from Black Sail Pass. Or you can walk leisurely along the old pony track on Moses' Sledgate from the top of Honister to Beck Head and thence fairly gently to the top. Most of the higher reaches of the mountain belong to the National Trust, being part of the climbers' war memorial land, and at the very foot of the mountain, in Mosedale, there is the memorial—if you can call it that—to the legendary Will Ritson—Ritson Force.

But Kirk Fell is not only a walkers' mountain and a pleasant viewpoint, for it is well skirted with crags on its northern side and these include Boat Howe, a useful climbing ground, first pioneered more than forty years ago. Boat Howe was doubtless so named because it has about it something of the shape of a boat and its central pillar—called 'The Boat'—is one of the finest pieces of clean, isolated rock in the Lake District. The pioneers gave the first climbs they made names like Sea Wall Arête, Starboard Chimney, the Hatchway, the Rigging, Coastguard

Climb and even The Bilge, and years after their discovery of these routes the impressive Prow of the Boat was first climbed. I remember many happy days on these climbs, where it is still possible to spend a quiet afternoon far from the queues for the Napes Needle and other popular ascents.

Another memory of Kirk Fell is of being lost on the top. It may seem surprising that four experienced mountaineers could be lost in summer-time on a modest peak like this, but it happened. We had been climbing on Boat Howe and at the end of the day, instead of going across to Beck Head and along the Sledgate to Honister, thought we might as well walk first over the summit of the mountain. It was misty but we didn't bother to get out our compasses. After all, we were only on Kirk Fell.

But there are hardly any tracks on Kirk Fell and what few there are seem to wander all round the mountain instead of across it, being mostly sheep trods. We went along one of these, imagining we were steering for the summit, or one of them, but we never reached any summit that day. After about half an hour of getting nowhere we decided we should do something about it, only to find that each one of us had different ideas about where we were. We led in turn and, I suppose, during the next hour or so must have covered most of the mountain. But we found no summit, no tarns, nothing. And maps and compasses were of course, useless, since we could not pinpoint where we were.

I can't remember how long we wandered over the mountain in the mist, but I do recall that we began to get tired for we had had a long day. We could only see a few yards ahead and we were feeling hungry, too. It was then decided to go straight downhill at the steepest place we could find so as to get below the mist as quickly as possible but risking a descent into Ennerdale, Mosedale or Wasdale. And after a time, the curtains of mist suddenly parted below us and we saw we were looking down on the familiar fields of Wasdale Head. We then had to traverse wearily round the Wasdale side of the mountain and climb all the way up again to Beck Head, so that it was four very tired, and humble, mountaineers that eventually trundled down to Honister. This shows how easy it is to go wrong on a mountain if you don't look where you're going—even if the mountain is only Kirk Fell.

So this neglected mountain has my respect as well as my affection—a wonderful place from which to survey the best of

Lakeland, but a mountain that is perhaps not quite so naïve as it looks. For even Kirk Fell—the mountain of the church, the little church of Wasdale Head—has its subtleties if you care to seek them out.

3

STEEP PLACES

(Some Western Hills)

Pillar

Perhaps the best view of Pillar is from the east when its soaring ridge looks like a wind-blown sail, but the mountain is not among the most impressive or photogenic in Lakeland. It has no characteristic shape and from some angles its summit looks little more than a hump on a high, steep ridge. A score of smaller Lakeland mountains are much more striking. But this big lump of fell blocking the head of Mosedale, or rearing up above the Ennerdale conifers, has one tremendous redeeming feature that establishes it as a fine mountain—the magnificent precipice of Pillar Rock from which the mountain takes its name.

It is impossible to write of Pillar without mentioning the Rock for this is the whole glory of the mountain and the glory of Ennerdale—the tallest mass of vertical crag in England, and the only precipice in Lakeland with a summit unattainable by the ordinary walker.

But although Pillar Rock is a much bigger affair than Blackpool Tower, and a thousand times more beautiful and inspiring, it is the least visited of the major crags of the Lake District and is probably completely unknown to the majority of casual visitors. Thousands of people who claim some familiarity with Lakeland have never even seen it, and many must have looked across the head of Ennerdale from the Buttermere fells without even noting the Rock which has a habit of blending into its background. And from the summits of most of the mountains of Lakeland, Pillar Rock is either unseen or unremarkable. Even from the summit of Pillar mountain it appears relatively insignificant, for you only see its short southern side and the tremendous drop down to the River Liza is not apparent.

Indeed, it is only when you approach the crags from the Forestry Commission plantations, or better still, along the High Level Route from Wasdale, that the great rock is seen in all its splendour. The toil up the fellside from the jungle of conifers is steep, and even here, immediately below the crag, the Rock is out of sight for part of the way but, half-way up, the great cone comes into view and, although greatly foreshortened, this sight of so much vertical rock can make a man feel very small indeed. But the perfect approach is along the High Level Route which contours along the Ennerdale side of Pillar, skirting little green coves, rising and falling across rocky ridges and then reaching Robinson's Cairn, the memorial to a great mountaineer and Lakeland lover. And this is the perfect viewpoint for the Rock.

It rises straight ahead, a great cathedral-like structure, but bigger than any cathedral in the world. A green ledge runs along its foot and above it the great walls rise almost vertically for about five hundred feet to Low Man, above which there is an upper section leading to High Man, the small summit. The crag is flanked by other crags, with scree slopes in between and there are only a handful of places in Britain—all of them in Scotland— where you can see more rock in one glance.

Viewed from this point it is easy to understand why the Rock has always been an object of awe to the dalesfolk, and why the earliest guides to Lakeland listed it as one of the district's most remarkable features. It was first climbed in 1826—fifty years before the start of the sport of rock-climbing—by an Ennerdale man named John Atkinson who probably reached the top by what is nowadays known as the Old West Route. This is little more than a scramble but Atkinson had to contend, not merely with the difficulties of the route, but also with the accumulated fears and prejudices of the age. Whether he felt any pride or awe at being the first to reach High Man we do not know, but as he looked down the long length of Ennerdale towards his home he must have felt a great exhilaration. For there is a great difference between the view from the average Lakeland summit and that from the top of the Rock. In the one case you are astraddle the rooftops; in the other, perched on the weather-vane of a church spire.

There are few more wonderful places in this country for the

enjoyment of an outdoor summer's evening than the top of the Rock. On many occasions I've perched up there, on a couch of ling or a coil of rope, enjoying all the advantages of being on top of a steeple without having to suffer the snags. Even the controversial Ennerdale conifers, 2,000 vertical feet below, look almost picturesque from this viewpoint and one can lazily watch the clouds slowly sailing over miles of distant fells without turning the head. No sounds reach you on top of the Rock, for you are much too high above the tumbling river and the water-falls and too remote from the sheep and the occasional slither of scree. Even the chatter of other climbers, out of sight and far below, is quite inaudible and you do not hear them until they suddenly appear over the edge from the unseen depths, first a hand and then a tousled mop of hair. Only the climbers can disturb your reverie on top of the Rock—except during August when you might also get the midges.

There are more than fifty climbing routes on Pillar Rock, ranging from easy scrambles like Slab and Notch to the extremely steep and exposed routes on the west face of High Man. You can reach the summit after five hundred feet of steep difficult climbing, or perhaps two hundred feet of moderate scrambling or even by routes only fifty feet in length. The only thing wrong with Pillar Rock from the climber's point of view is that its southern side, although vertical, is far too short, but just the right height for dropping into Jordan Gap on a doubled rope. The collapse of the boulders in the gap would transform the Rock and give it the real isolation it deserves.

Many famous names—including Haskett Smith, J. W. Robinson, O. G. Jones, the Abraham brothers and H. M. Kelly—have been associated with the development of Pillar Rock as a climbing ground, and there has also been the occasional eccentric. One of these was the Rev. James Jackson, the self-styled Patriarch of the Pillarites who climbed the Rock when in his eightieth year. Three years later he was found dead below Great Doup, having apparently fallen several hundred feet. 'Steeple' Jackson, as he was also known after he had repaired the weathercock of his own church, was a great walker, a formidable personality and obviously, since his ascent was made as long ago as 1875, a man of considerable courage.

Shepherds must have known the neighbourhood of Pillar Rock for centuries. Sheep have a habit of working down a fellside in search of grazing and through the years hundreds of them must have wandered down from Pillar to the Rock and then fallen to their deaths down such places as Walker's Gully and Shamrock Gully. From time to time short stretches of wall have been built above the gullies to try and prevent these accidents but every year tragic remains are found at the foot of the precipice. And up to two hundred years ago the sheep on Pillar faced another risk—that of being forked off the ledges above the Rock by the antlers of red deer who objected to intruders in what was then their sanctuary.

Wedge-shaped Pillar mountain is a steep fell all round— quite apart from the verticalities of the Rock—and must be counted among the steepest and roughest mountains in Lakeland. The Ennerdale side, skirted with conifers on the lower slopes, is a formidable grind when the mountain is being tackled from the Liza after the walk over Scarth Gap from Buttermere, and the opposite side overlooking Mosedale is, in effect, a mountain wall. Only along the ridge from Looking Stead is the mountain gently sloped and this is one of the routes from Black Sail.

I remember one amusing experience many, many years ago at the head of this pass. We were on our way to climb on Pillar Rock, although it was pouring with rain and the mist so thick we could barely see a yard or two ahead. Nowadays we wouldn't dream of going climbing in these sort of conditions, but we were very young and very keen in those days. Somewhere near the head of the pass we'd stopped to eat a sodden sandwich or two in the lee of a dripping rock and were very startled indeed to hear, out of the mist and rain and almost at our elbows, a plaintive voice asking, of all things, if the speaker was on the correct road to Whitehaven. And then, out of the misty downpour, loomed a strange bedraggled figure—with a bicycle across his back. We had thought we were practically the only people about on the Lakeland fells and here was a cyclist carrying his machine over mountains. I think we gave the determined fellow a bit of chocolate and sent him down into Mosedale with clear directions for the Gosforth road, and our very best wishes. I hope he made it all right.

At the other end of the Pillar summit ridge is the high col of Wind Gap. This little dip in the ridge separates the mountain from Steeple and between the two there is another rash of fine crags, high up on the fellside. The summit of Pillar may be won from this gap if the walker continues leftwards up Mosedale on his way from Wasdale Head instead of veering right along the well-scratched Black Sail route. It is also an excellent way down

Pillar from Ennerdale (Pillar Rock, partly caught by sunlight, is immediately below the summit)
Scoat Fell and Steeple above Mirk Cove (overleaf)

the mountain—to either Wasdale or Ennerdale—or you may continue over Steeple and Red Pike—a fine upland walk. These are picturesque mountain names—The Pillar, The Steeple and, a little further west, The Haycock, and this is magnificent walking country—rarely over-populated, and set high and steep above deep-set valleys.

For me, Pillar will always be the mountain of the Rock, but its steepness, bulk and height also make it a worthy fell in its own right. It may be unimpressive in shape, with no tarns in its corries, a man-made forest at its foot, and little colour on its slopes but it is still the King of the Mosedale fells and the highest mountain west of Great Gable. And no Lakeland mountain has a finer northern face, for on this side is perched The Rock.

Steeple

You could argue that Steeple, the mountain with the wonderful name and the fine ridge dipping down into Ennerdale, is really hardly a mountain at all. For purists will tell you it is only a spur of Scoat Fell connected by a short arête to the parent mountain which is not only higher and bulkier but also completely dominates its offshoot from many viewpoints. But Steeple, looking down into steep coves where the ravens fly and where the pine marten may have his home and then down the long length of Ennerdale and its conifers, will always be a mountain to me. For you feel you have got somewhere when you stand beside its scattered cairn with the ground dropping sharply below your feet and your eyes can take in at a glance some of the wildest scenery in England.

One of the many good things about Steeple is its name. Some Lakeland mountains—Glaramara, Blencathra, Grey Friar and Catbells are examples—have lovely romantic names that trip musically off the tongue and can bring back memories of the wind on the heights to men marooned in cities. Other mountain names—Robinson, perhaps, or Sheffield Pike or Watson's Dodd —seem rather dull, and tops like Low Pike never sound particularly exciting.

But there are two Lakeland mountains—next door to one another, as it happens—whose names, thought up by shepherds hundreds of years ago, seem exactly right. Pillar, the mountain of the Rock, and Steeple. Pillar Rock, bigger and more impressive than any cathedral, leans, all seven hundred feet of it,

4

The Screes above Wastwater (showing Great and C Gullies)
Harrison Stickle and Stickle Tarn (facing)

against the steep north face of its mountain and perhaps a mile away to the west is the sharp prow of the Steeple. And, viewed from the right angle it looks exactly like its name—a church steeple but bigger than any steeple you've ever seen.

The trouble, of course, with Steeple is that it's not like a steeple on all sides; if it was, it would be the most remarkable mountain in Britain. Just as the collapse of the boulders in Jordan Gap would transform Pillar Rock and tremendously increase its remoteness, so would a steepening of the gentle west ridge of Steeple vastly improve our mountain. But mountain fashioning is not for Man. It is just unfortunate for those of us who like our mountains to be shaped like the ones drawn by our children that the 'back' of Steeple—the Wasdale side—is not very remarkable, being no more than an incident on a ridge. But from the Ennerdale side, and especially when viewed from the crags to the east, the mountain suddenly asserts itself and the full dramatic splendour of its shape can be enjoyed.

I think my first sight of Steeple—or more correctly, Scoat Fell—was from Burnmoor when walking over to Wasdale as a boy, and I remember I was disappointed. I knew that Pillar Rock and Steeple were tremendously steep and craggy places but from the back the area looked very ordinary. But later I got to know the mountain quite well, for we often came back that way after a day's climbing on Pillar Rock, and with knowledge of its shape and character came affection. For this wild country to the west of Pillar is among the least frequented parts of Lakeland and its remoteness, the steepness of its rugged northern corries and the sunset views to the west give it a charm that is lacking from some of the better known parts of Lakeland. Mostly, we passed over the mountain in the early evening so Steeple is, for me, one of the sunset hills.

Sometimes, though, we went up to Steeple by way of Mosedale, the quiet, secluded valley under the crags of Red Pike, perhaps climbing on Elliptical Crag or doing problems on the curious split boulder on the way up, and occasionally we went by way of Wind Gap, the wild col between Scoat Fell and Pillar. The walk over Red Pike, Scoat Fell, Steeple and Pillar is one of the finest ridge walks in Lakeland.

Mountain nomenclature around these parts, although strikingly descriptive in the case of Pillar and Steeple, can also be curious. Scoat Fell has three summits, the most easterly being nameless but next to it is the highest point of the mountain and this is named Little Scoat Fell. And Great Scoat Fell, further to the west, is lower. The reason for this apparent mix-up is that the terms 'great' and 'little' refer not to the heights but rather to the area of the tops. Many maps give no height for Great Scoat Fell and some even miss out Little Scoat Fell which is the highest point on the range, apart from Pillar.

The late H. H. Symonds got quite worked up about this, criticizing the Ordnance Survey and Bartholomew and then adding: "I give it up. Personally, I name it Scoatfell, Scoatfell simple without prefix, suffix or hesitation. For Scoatfell it is, and its height is 2,746, and the Steeple is north of it and a spur of it, and a very good spur and is approximately fifty-seven feet lower at its highest point, and that's the end of it." But I'm afraid it isn't for the highest point of Scoat Fell (I prefer two words) is 2,760 feet and Steeple is seventy-three feet lower, although perhaps it doesn't matter very much.

There's also some confusion about Wind Gap, the col between Scoat Fell and Pillar for some maps call it Windy Gap, which is the name more correctly applied to the gap between Great Gable and Green Gable. Some years before the last war three or four climbers spent eleven days camping in Wind Gap or rather in the cove just below the col on the Ennerdale side and produced about a dozen new climbs on Black Crag, the fine precipice just to the east of Steeple.

Wind Gap Cove is a fine, upland corrie ringed by a half-mile cirque of crags. This is real mountain country and it is only one of a whole series of coves that flank the Ennerdale side of the Pillar range. Mirk Cove, separating Steeple from Scoat Fell, is perhaps the wildest of them, but there are also Hind Cove, Pillar Cove, Mirklin Cove, Silver Cove and Great Cove—all wonderful wild places little visited by the tourist.

I understand the word 'scoat' in Scoat Fell is an Old Norse word meaning something that juts or projects so that perhaps the peak namers had in mind Steeple itself, for the main fell is not remarkably abrupt or projecting. So that both the Viking settlers and the shepherds who named the Steeple were thinking of the same place—the steeply jutting crag that almost misses being a mountain.

Scoat Fell has two tarns—Scoat Tarn to the south, one of the finest of the western tarns, and Tewit How Tarn on the Ennerdale side, an irregularly-shaped pool in the peat moss with little beaches and promontories among the heather. Steeple itself has no tarns but has the twin streams of High Beck and Low Beck tumbling down in delightful cascades to the Liza. But first they have to flow through the conifers that long ago changed the look of Ennerdale for ever.

The summit of Steeple is a splendid viewpoint for the steep drop into the coves and the long sweep of Ennerdale are tremendously impressive. This is the real glory of this sharp little peak—the sight of the wild, rocky corries below your feet and the feeling of airiness that the climber often experiences but the walker only rarely. The situation, of course, is much more dramatic when you are perched on the top of Pillar Rock but while the Rock is only accessible to the climber the Steeple may be easily reached by the most cautious of walkers, without once using the hands. He may even walk on and off the crag in thick mist—if he knows where he is going—so perhaps Steeple is the pedestrian's Pillar Rock, with much the same views, the same absence of orange peel and litter, and afterwards the same glorious walk back to Wasdale or Ennerdale. And when the popular summits are overrun with the summer crowds there'll generally be peace enough on Steeple to sit and watch the ravens.

Yewbarrow

My first acquaintance with Yewbarrow must have been in the early 1930s when we used to run down the screes of Dore Head at the northern end of the peak as a suitably flourishing ending to a day's climbing on Pillar Rock. We thought this the finest scree run in the Lake District and perhaps it was, but it is now useless as a means of quick descent, all the stones having been rolled and washed away. Perhaps Great Hell Gate on Gable will go the same way in time.

Since then I've been on the mountain many times but it was only on my last visit, a year or two ago, that I realized how steep Yewbarrow is—on all sides. Perhaps I'm getting old, but I can't think of any other mountain as small as this one and yet so steep all round. Undoubtedly, for all its modest height—little more than two thousand feet—Yewbarrow is a real mountain, with much more than its fair share of crag, a fine cock's comb of a ridge and some of the most exciting summit views in Lakeland. For from its craggy top you can look down into perhaps the finest dale-head in the district or across at the cliffs of Scafell, or turn round and peer down into the depths of Wastwater. This last is one of the great attractions of Yewbarrow— the sight of the dark lake below your feet and, in the distance, the sea, so that you might be high up in the Cuillins looking across Hebridean waters.

Indeed, little Yewbarrow has much of the character of a Cuillin peak. For its long, narrow summit is ringed with crag on both sides and cleft here and there by dark gullies, while each end of the ridge is protected by cliff. So that the traverse of the mountain, if you keep on the ridge all the way, is more of a climb than a scramble and beyond the compass of ordinary walkers. And not many Lakeland summits are protected in this way.

My last visit was on a Bank Holiday, and I was merely seizing the chance of a couple of hours' exercise on a lazy family outing. Most Bank Holidays I keep well away from Lakeland, preferring solitude to crowds, but this day we had seen little traffic along the Cumberland coast and I had been tempted to drive into Wasdale. And having got so far it seemed almost sacrilege to be motoring in such surroundings so I stopped the car and strolled up Yewbarrow to stretch my legs and savour the heights.

It must have been four or five years since I had last been up Yewbarrow and I had forgotten it is such a rocky place. I kept straight up the ridge of Bell Rib and when I reached the crag was glad I had left my dog Sambo with the family at the foot of the fell. He is well accustomed to steep places but not so steep as this. Perhaps this is no place for a solitary climber, but I had been there before and worked my way up the final wall and chimneys with considerable care.

As I went higher there were fascinating peeps across to Burnmoor Tarn and, to the left, the lonely pool of Low Tarn underneath Red Pike, and when I finally reached the top there was Gable to the right and Pillar straight ahead, and the fields of Wasdale Head far below and deeply carved valleys all around. Almost the perfect grandstand, this ridge, with the finest mountains in England—Pillar, Gable and the Scafells—in a ring all round you and the heart of mountain Lakeland two thousand feet below your boots. There were tiny pockets of snow still hanging in the hills and a stiff breeze was sending the cloud shadows racing across the sunlit slopes but the picture was not quite the same as I remembered it long ago. For the head of Wasdale, just beyond the lake, was a gaily coloured patchwork of tents—blue, yellow, red, all the colours of the rainbow—and some of the mystery of the secret valley of our youth seemed to have disappeared. What a pity, I thought, they couldn't have sited this camping ground in the woods at the other end of the lake, and left the dale-head unspoiled. Surely the campers would not have been too far from the fells. The early climbers walked all the way from the railway at Seascale and didn't think that Scafell was too far away. But perhaps I was being selfish for here was I climbing a mountain from a car at the foot. I suppose one must move with the times.

Yewbarrow rightly takes its place among the Wasdale giants. Its wedge shape is prominent in the foreground as you drive north-eastwards up the dale and the fell is the real guardian of the shrine of Wasdale Head. You drive round its skirts as you approach the sanctuary and the hotel is perched at its foot. The broom on the craggy bluffs of the fell makes a brave show and the waters of the lake lap its feet. Mosedale Beck and Over Beck almost ring the mountain on other sides so that the fell stands alone with the scramble of Stirrup Crag above Dore Head separating it from its nearest neighbour, Red Pike. The little valley of Over Beck above Bowderdale Farm is one of the gems of Lakeland and overhanging the valley is the cliff of Overbeck Crag or Dropping Crag, nowadays criss-crossed with climbing routes. This is a good place to take beginners, and is a better practice ground than the upper cliffs of Bell Rib.

From the crag you can run down the band to Bowderdale in a few minutes. On my last visit I met a disconsolate couple on the way down who asked me how one got up the mountain. They had tried what seemed to them the straightforward way over Bell Rib but had been turned back by the crags and couldn't see another way. I suggested the tourist route beyond Overbeck Crag and they said they would try it as they wanted to look down on Wasdale and across to Pillar. I thought it rather wonderful that here was a little mountain, right in the very heart of things, but without a really easy way up and by no means over-scratched with tracks. Yewbarrow stands nearer the heart of mountain Lakeland than any other fell and yet is still unspoiled by the hordes and remains a challenging little peak of considerable character.

The Screes

The most dramatic mountain view in England for the motorist is not the sight of the Scafells or Helvellyn, nor the ridges of Blencathra nor the crags of Great Gable, nor even the rock turrets of the Langdale Pikes. No, the most breath-taking mountain picture in Lakeland to be seen from the roadway is probably the north-west front of Whin Rigg and the western slopes of Illgill Head.

Strangely unfamiliar mountain names to some of you, perhaps. They're only small mountains—not much more than half the height of Scafell Pike—but your first view of them as you drive through the woods near Wasdale Hall towards the grandest dale-head in England, if you have picked the right day, can pull you up in yards. We call them, more familiarly, the Wastwater Screes or, as often as not, just 'The Screes'.

They rise perhaps fifteen hundred feet within the space of less than half a mile from the farther shore of England's deepest lake—vast tilted rivers of scree poised steeply above the lake and capped by wild crags savagely split by dark, vertical ravines. Seen through the trees at the seaward end of the lake, especially in autumn or winter, the colours are really exciting—the russet tints of the dead bracken, the red streaks of iron-ore in the crags and screes, the rich dark umber of the precipices, and the green, brown and purple splashes of the hanging gardens caught among the rocks.

The picture is always changing according to the lighting and the time of year. Below, Wastwater may be dark and brooding, storm-tossed and flecked white with driven spray, or sparkling in the sunlight, and the lake's moods will be echoed on the mountain wall. But no matter the weather the overall effect is always dramatic and inspiring, and sometimes even awesome. Here, among fantastic minarets of rock and black cavernous gullies, could be the abode of trolls.

Nowhere else in Lakeland can such a splendid chaos of rock and scree—nearly two miles of it—be seen from the roadway; nowhere else in England is there such an exciting 'surprise view' as this. See this mountain wall lit by the evening sun, or towards the end of a short winter's afternoon, with the rain stopped and the rocks glistening, or perhaps some patches of snow hanging in the gullies, and you have caught a view that can stand comparison—in dramatic quality—with many of the much-vaunted continental mountain scenes.

But I must not give the impression that the Screes are only to be enjoyed by the motorist for, indeed, the rewards for the walker and climber are far, far greater. You may walk along the screes themselves and under the crags, or along the ridge on top of the precipices, or you may climb the crags by one of the gullies. Or you can walk up to the top of the ridge from either end of the lake, or from Burnmoor, or from lonely Miterdale, or you may merely study the line of cliffs from the opposite side of the lake.

Over the years I've managed to do all these things, some of them many times, so that now I feel justified in suggesting that, for their height, these must be the most satisfying 'little hills' in Lakeland. And undoubtedly one of their most rewarding features is the walk along the length of the ridge—a simple, airy expedition providing magnificent views of Wasdale Head and the central mountains of Lakeland in one direction, and the sea and the concrete towers of Calder Hall in the other.

The real thrill of the walk is the wonderful view of the whole length of Wastwater, seemingly almost vertically below, the toy houses and farms at Strands and Nether Wasdale, and, best of all, the peeps down the gullies, and down into the crazy, rock scenery. For some of it *does* look rather crazy—huge crumbling pillars poised fantastically above the lake and ready to fall, although I've no doubt some of them have looked just like this for thousands of years. But a few years ago one of these shattered rock towers *did* crash down the screes into the lake with a noise heard miles away, and within a few moments, completely altered the appearance of this part of the mountain wall. Even so, you can keep right to the edge of the cliffs to get the best out of this walk. The rock falls take place below the summit ridge and there's no danger of falling over, even for those prone to dizziness.

When you look at the Screes from below, the ridge looks long and almost level but in fact there are two summits. The higher is Illgill Head, nearly two thousand feet above sea-level, and rises about half-way along Wastwater. The other, the right-hand summit as seen from the lake shore, is Whin Rigg, more than two hundred feet lower, and just opposite Wasdale Hall at the western end of the lake. Between the two summits lies the Screes, the name loosely given to the whole ridge which should really only be applied to the steep portion of crag and fellside dropping steeply to the lake. To some people the scree slopes may look perpendicular, although I believe they are no steeper than forty-five degrees, but the crags above are certainly steep enough and soar to the vertical in places. They say that the scree continues at the same steepness down to the bottom of the lake— you can check this on the six-inch Ordnance Survey map—and the lake sinks to a depth of 258 feet, the deepest inland gulf in the country. The bottom, immediately beneath Illgill Head, touches well below sea-level.

Up on the ridge, half-way between the two summits is a small peaty tarn, with a smaller one beside it, and eastwards the slope falls away easily into the little-visited valley of Miterdale and down by the Whillan Beck to the valley of the Esk. Of the two summit views, that from Illgill Head is possibly the finer, with its rather more intimate panorama of the Wasdale hills, but the more dramatic view is the Whin Rigg picture of the shattered profile of the Screes plunging down into the dark depths of Wastwater.

Several times I've been to the Screes to climb. Of the two main gullies falling down from Whin Rigg towards the lake, the one on the left, as seen from Wasdale Hall, is the longer and is called Great Gully, while the one a little further to the right is C Gully. Both provide magnificent severe rock climbs and each time I've been there, no matter what the weather, the pitches have been wet, sometimes with waterfalls pouring down them. The last time I was in Great Gully we had just emerged, wet through and rather dirty, from the top pitch and were coiling the rope when a fox got up almost underneath our feet and ran streaking through the heather and the bracken down towards the Irt.

Great Gully has seventeen pitches, and the remains of an aeroplane are embedded among the rocks below the first one. Both climbs are among the most rewarding of their type in Lakeland. The rock scenery is strikingly dramatic, with fine amphitheatres as you progress up the crag, but the crumbling, iron-spattered rock on the vegetation-covered walls has so far discouraged much exploration outside the gullies, although one or two routes have been pioneered in recent years. But the crags are certainly among the least explored of the bigger precipices of Lakeland and there still remain big areas of probably treacherous rock where no man has ever been.

Most Lake District visitors, however, don't climb rocks and an easier expedition for the average person might be the traverse of the lakeside path which goes underneath the crags and along the screes. This trip has been variously described as 'impossible' or 'very easy'. For the average performer it is a perfectly feasible ramble although at one point it is rather rough and becomes a bit of a scramble. Early guide-books described this as a very dangerous expedition, claiming that one risked being struck by boulders trundling down the screes but this is, of course, nonsense. Nobody was hurt by the tremendous fall a few years ago and, indeed, nobody saw it happen. The chances of another fall occurring as you happen to be walking along are sufficiently remote to be discounted. You must be careful at one place but it can be managed, if necessary, on a wild, wet night with a poorish torch, as two of us once discovered.

One interesting feature of the Screes is the big slice carved out of the fellside about half a mile to the west of the summit of Whin Rigg—Great Hall Gill. It is rather like a long crater running down from the ridge and is quite unlike anywhere else in the district. The gill seems to have been formed by the crumbling of a band of granite leaving curious rock fingers, pink scree and strange banks of sand. In between are stretches of grass, bubbling streams, pleasant ledges and sheep-trods, making the ravine a rather strange, other-worldly sort of place. Iron used to be worked there at one time, I believe.

My last visit to the Screes was to one of the gullies which we found even wetter and greasier than usual. Holds were masked with bright green moss and slime, water sprayed off the gully walls and we clawed our way up cool, dank chimneys in murky gloom. But outside, framed by the black streaming walls we could see the lake far below and a segment of rather unfamiliar sunlit countryside. For it's a different country around the Screes and it's still not so well known. Years ago I used to think that the Screes were only really worth visiting when the day was too wet and miserable for anything more worthwhile—a trudge round the lake and over the ridge in the rain, just for the exercise. But, with advancing years and much less energy I think it's a place to visit for its own sake—a place where you can get right away from the summer crowds and see sights and views quite different from those in any other part of Lakeland.

4

FAMILIAR FELLS

(Around Langdale)

Langdale Pikes

Fifteen miles away as the raven flies, neatly framed in my study window between a Scots pine and a battered old yew, is the battlemented profile of the Langdale Pikes, sharply etched in blue against a changing sky. Every day, except when the clouds are down, I can admire their familiar shape, and it is so easy in imagination to reach out and draw them nearer. So easy to picture the homely dale with its ring of encircling fells—the perfection, to thousands of people, of Lakeland mountain charm and sculptured grandeur.

In half an hour, perhaps, I can reach the dale, but, in imagination, I can be there in a moment—with a choice of a hundred different memories and a score of changing views. Most often I think of the evenings and especially those long, sunlit, golden evenings in early summer when we have come running down from the crags into the great bowl of the dale, loud with the clamour of sheep and their young lambs. There are long shadows across the lovely turf in Mickleden, the notched line of the Crinkles and Bowfell is dark against the sunset, but the evening sun lights up the steep front of Gimmer and the west-facing crags, dances down the beck, and glows on the farmhouse roofs. The dale is dotted white with the grazing sheep and the noise of their bleating—sometimes a deep-throated 'baa', and then a high-pitched cry of alarm, and then a whole chorus of sorrowful chords—fills the dale. It is the most peaceful scene in the world and one of the oldest in history, and perhaps we pause in our helter-skelter dash down the dusty screes to a long, cool drink in a shadowed bar, and let the sheer contentment of it all seep into our souls. There is nobody else about—only the sheep and ravens recklessly quartering the sky, and, down by the beck, a flicker of arms and legs across the pool.

But there are many other Langdale memories—crisp winter mornings with the sun glinting on the snow-filled gullies of Crinkle Crags, days of high adventure on the north-west precipice of Gimmer, an evening bathe in Stickle Tarn, or just the crisp smell of breakfast bacon outside the tent after a splash in the beck, or the stroll down the lane to supper in a candle-lit room.

For me Langdale will always be the mountains and crags, the happy companionship of youthful days, sparkling mornings meant for high endeavour, and the hills as they go to sleep on golden summer evenings. And, indeed, for most of us the attraction of the dale, despite the long story of the quarries and the gunpowder works, the pastoral charm of its long, level floor, the waterfalls, and even the stone-axe 'factory' above the screes, is principally the skyline—the most photographed and most easily recognized group of hills in England.

The fells of Lakeland, although often unsurpassed in quiet beauty, are by no means always striking or dramatic in form. Sometimes, indeed, they rise as almost shapeless humps, their fine ridges or great crags hidden from the casual viewer, so that the highest mountain in England appears from many angles as a rather dull lump of fell, and the first sight of Helvellyn from the Kendal to Keswick road must have disappointed thousands. But the Langdale hills are different. As mountains go they are small but they assume, when viewed from most sides except the north, the sort of jagged shape more often associated with the northern Highlands or the Western Isles. They rise in turreted splendour from the level floor of one of the most perfect valleys in England and although they may only be little hills they *look* like mountains. Yesterday, perhaps, the clouds hung about their summit crags, but this morning the square towers gleamed in the sunlight and, as I write, I can still see their shape, purple against the sunset.

Towards the north the Pikes tail away into the featureless slopes of High Raise and Sergeant Man but right down the dale they present the view pictured on a million postcards—all straight lines and right-angles with shadows perhaps where the crags lie, and an impression of rugged strength and dignity. The shape of a crouching lion, if you like, guarding a scene of quiet, pastoral repose.

Men have been climbing on these crags since before the turn of the century, but other men were here before the dawn of history, four thousand years ago, fashioning their axe-heads and other weapons and tools from the rocks lying below the cliffs. I use one of these axe-heads, picked up on the screes below Pike o' Stickle a dozen years ago, as a paper-weight. The lovely green rock is still as sharp as when it was first chipped out by one of these early men, and you can still admire his craftsmanship.

The biggest crag in the area is Pavey Ark which towers, rather like a hanging garden, over the nearly circular Stickle Tarn, where, in season, one may bathe, fish or skate. Pavey Ark is the right-hand shoulder of the highest turret, Harrison Stickle, as viewed from Lowwood or on your way up the dale. It was the first of the crags to be 'discovered' by the climbers and has its share of fine routes, but the finest crag in the area is Gimmer Crag—the left-hand edge of Loft Crag, the next peak leftwards of Harrison Stickle. From the valley this precipice appears of little significance and not nearly so impressive as the striking-looking Pike o' Stickle that sticks up, further left still, like a great rocky thumb set on a towering ridge. But there is no climbing to speak of on the Sugar Loaf, as it is sometimes called, although the peak lends itself to photography and is an airy viewpoint.

Gimmer, however, is a wonderful crag, one of the finest for steepness and exposure in Lakeland. It rears skywards, smooth and perpendicular in places, full in the sunshine all day long, and completely free from vegetation. The fellside below falls extremely steeply to the valley so that when you are perched high up on the face you feel remote as on a church steeple, but with a bigger drop below, and a much better view all round. There are not many places in Lakeland where the climber, engaged on routes of no more than average difficulty, can taste the delights of verticality more satisfactorily than on Gimmer. The rock is wonderfully hard and firm, although rather lacking in suitable belays, and the fly-on-a-wall feeling is enhanced by the fact that the face approaches the vertical as it nears the top. The whole front of the crag is a maze of fine, airy routes, comparatively little scratched—for Gimmer was never a very popular place in nailed boots—and round the corner to the left, on the north-west face, there are harder and even steeper climbs, including some of the most testing in Lakeland. And when you have reached the top of most of these Gimmer climbs you can, at the right time of year, take your ease on couches of sweet-smelling bilberry, refresh yourself with their luscious fruit, and look out over half of Lakeland.

But Langdale is not only for the adventurer seeking the heights; its mountains may be the main attraction but there is much else besides. We think of Langdale as the valley threaded by the Great Langdale Beck but there is also Little Langdale and the Brathay, on the other side of the winding Blea Tarn road, while the main valley splits into two beyond Dungeon Ghyll. Perhaps there could be no greater contrast in neighbouring valleys than that in Mickleden and Oxendale—the one, level-floored and turf carpeted right to its head and threaded by its quiet beck, and the other, just over the shoulder of the Band, wild, tumbled, little-visited, carved into deep ravines, and loud with the noise of waterfalls. All this is Langdale, the quietness and the clamour, the rocky heights and the lush turf of the intake fields, seclusion in wild places and queues for beer or afternoon tea at the popular hotels. Everybody goes to Langdale—the climber, the walker, the motorist bound for the Blea Tarn road, the axe-head collector, the tourist seeking a good meal, and those who like to see a good waterfall. Nearly a hundred years ago John Ruskin came to Langdale and found "the loveliest rock scenery, chased with silver waterfalls that I ever set foot or heart upon. The Swiss torrent-beds are always more or less savage and ruinous, with a terrible sense of overpowering strength and danger, lulled. But here, the sweet heather and ferns and star-mosses nestled in close to the dashing of the narrow streams, while every cranny of crag held its own little placid lake of amber, trembling with falling drops. . . . What a place for a hot afternoon after five, with no wind, and absolute solitude; no creature, except a lamb or two, to mix any ruder sound or voice with the splash of the innumerable streamlets!"

Dungeon Ghyll, in its lower reaches, is the haunt of the cautious tourist in high heels or carrying an umbrella, but higher up the ravine the more agile explorer will find a winding, upland mile of remarkably varied and even exciting scenery. Here, by the upper falls, he can escape the crowds and the orange peel—as he may also do in a dozen places in Oxendale—and discover for himself a little bit of the real Lakeland. And overlooking all this wonderland of rock and water, the slopes of heather, bracken, bilberry and juniper, and the magic of golden mornings and long, still evenings, are the Langdale Pikes—guardians of the sanctuary, changeless in a thousand years, but new every morning to those who worship here.

Bowfell

Bowfell is undoubtedly one of the finest mountains in Lakeland —a shy but shapely pyramid, without notoriety or glamour, stuck right in the centre of some of the best country in England. An honest mountain quite devoid of guile, you might say—unless you happen to be using a compass near Ore Gap.

Bowfell is one of the easiest mountains in the Lake District to recognize and is visible, unmasked by other peaks, from almost all sides. You can see it from the fell at the back of my house—a shapely cone at the end of a ridge—and it is equally visible from mountain tops, from many of the valleys, from places around the coast, and even from some of the towns. Norman Nicholson has written of Bowfell—one of the few references by modern writers: "Walking in a mining town by the sea you turn a corner, and there, at the end of the street, between the gasworks and the Roman Catholic Chapel, miles away across the marshes, is Bowfell."

The mountain is easy to recognize because, unlike most Lakeland peaks, its summit has the traditional shape—an equilateral triangle. If you ask a child to draw a mountain it will show you something like the top of Bowfell. Stickle Pike in Dunnerdale has much the same shape, so have two or three mountains in North Wales, so—much more dramatically—has the Matterhorn, but not very many Lakeland mountain tops are so traditional in shape. Grisedale Pike might sometimes qualify but, as often not, is hidden by other tops. The best-known mountain shape in Lakeland—the Langdale Pikes—is unrecognizable from 'the back' to the uninitiated, while the sugar-loaf shape of Great Gable is lost when not seen end-on. Scafell Pike, the highest mountain in England, has no real characteristic shape; Harter Fell in Cumberland often looks a better peak. But Bowfell looks properly conical from all directions, even if the cone appears stuck on the end of a ridge. It is a big mountain—not far short of three thousand feet—and a mountain with a shape you can recognize from most parts of Lakeland.

Almost the only thing some guide-books say about Bowfell is that there is magnetic rock on the summit, so that compasses are unreliable, but this is more confusing than helpful. The facts are that minor variations of one or two degrees may be found at a number of points between Crinkle Crags and Esk Pike and about three degrees near Shelter Crags, but in every case you have to hold your compass close to the rock for the deviation to be observed. But on the north-west side of Ore Gap you can get deviations of up to 170 degrees on certain rocks if you place your compass in the right place, so that compasses used in this way could send you back the way you had come. It was the Brathay Exploration Group who reached these conclusions after a most detailed survey carried out several years ago, and it seems clear from their report that all you have to do to avoid being misled by your compass on Bowfell is simply to make sure you don't place the thing on a rock or very close to one.

Otherwise Bowfell is a perfectly straightforward mountain with crags where you'd expect to find them—on the north and east sides—and well sculptured, easily identified shoulders. Ore Gap, where the highly magnetized rocks appear to be, has probably been in use as a pass for at least two thousand years— the stone-axes from Pike o' Stickle probably went this way— and Three Tarns (there are five of them, really) are difficult to mistake.

Bowfell, like most good mountains, is a rock mountain in its upper tiers and the rock runs to crags in many places. Over the years I have spent dozens of happy hours on the climbs on Bowfell Buttress and elsewhere and many a winter's day in the ice packed gullies in its north-east corner. The Great Slab on Flat Crags is quite unlike anything seen anywhere else in Lakeland and walkers anxious to get the feel of the mountain can traverse it quite easily. Not far away from the summit plateau, perhaps about three hundred yards north-east of the cairn and between the crag of the Cambridge Climb and Hanging Knotts, there used to be, crouched among the rocks, a crudely built stone hut about eight feet square with a stone roof. It commanded a splendid view down Mickleden, and I have heard it suggested that it might have been a smugglers' hut, perched in this rather inaccessible place so that the men could watch the valleys and the passes for signs of the excisemen. How much of this is true— or indeed whether the hut is still there, for I haven't explored these rocks for years—I can't say. One suggestion is that the hut might have been associated with the enterprises of the legendary Moses Rigg, who is said to have used the hut on Gable Crag— now in ruins—but the activities of this former quarryman have never, to the best of my knowledge, been properly authenticated,

Scafell, Scafell Pike, Esk Pike and Bowfell (Hardknott Fort may be seen in the left foreground)
Crinkle Crags and Oxendale (overleaf)

and it would, perhaps, be unfair, to credit him with hide-outs on half the crags in Lakeland. Perhaps the Bowfell hut was no more than a shepherds' shelter—although in rather an out-of-the-way place. I would welcome any real information from an authority on these matters.

As a mountain of character Bowfell rightly lords it over two Lakeland counties, for the summit ridge lies on the Cumberland-Westmorland boundary. It rises at the head of three of the finest valleys in Lakeland—Langdale, Eskdale and Langstrath— and its waters run down these valleys into Windermere, Derwentwater and the sea. Below the terraced cliffs of Hanging Knotts, in a dark hollow, is the finely situated Angle Tarn, where I once enjoyed a 6 a.m. bathe. We had camped the previous night by the shore of the tarn in heavy, driving rain and had spent most of the night in sodden sleeping bags, trying to stop the tent from being blown away. But the dawn was sheer magic. Gone was the gloom so often associated with this dark hollow, for instead the morning sunlight was sparkling across the waters and our figures cast long shadows across the turf. After our weary night a bathe was irresistible and we were splashing in even before we had put out the sleeping bags to dry. And after that the bacon and eggs, on the morning of a day that turned out to be one of the hottest of the year, tasted quite wonderful.

If you pick the right day the view from the summit of Bowfell can be unequalled in Lakeland. Scotland can sometimes be seen and often the Solway Firth, the estuaries of the Esk and Duddon, the Northern Pennines and the Yorkshire hills and almost all the mountains in Lakeland. There is a splendid close-up view of the Scafells, and if there is snow about and the skies have their winter clarity the effect of airy isolation above a great white world is magical.

Although Bowfell can be ascended from all directions, including Hell Gill out of Oxendale, I have never found the mountain so swarming with hordes of people as Helvellyn, Gable and Scafell Pike so often are, nor is it unduly littered with cairns. And it is a friendly mountain with a low accident rate. Rock-climbers, tired of queuing up for the climbs on Gimmer or Raven Crag find the rocks on Bowfell a pleasant change—not very sunny and often wet, but never crowded and always with a considerable character of their own. And it is often worth the extra walk to get well away, out of sight and sound of the cars roaring up and down the Blea Tarn road.

5

The summit of High Raise (Great End on left skyline and Great Gable to the right)
The summit of Helm Crag (facing)

Some of the early scrambling routes on Bowfell were among the earliest rock-climbs in Lakeland. Haskett Smith went up the North Gully on Bowfell Buttress in 1882 and the curious Bowfell Links round the other side of the mountain were climbed by the Abrahams and others before the turn of the century. The Buttress itself, one of the best standard 'difficults' in Lakeland was first climbed in 1902 and since then hundreds of climbers, thinking they were coping with an ordinary straightforward route, have been brought up short by the awkwardness of the crack on the fifth pitch. Of course, there are any number of very much harder climbs on the mountain—and also some interesting nomenclature. Borstal Buttress, for instance, is situated on the crag of the Cambridge Climb, while just below the summit of the Band leading up to the summit pyramid you have the Neckband, then, a year or two later, Nectar, and then, later still, The Gizzard, although The Gullett might have been more anatomically appropriate.

Two of us once spent a winter's afternoon hacking through a snow-cornice at the top of one of the Bowfell gullies and I remember how cold it was working in the shadow under the overhanging snow. But finally we pulled out over the cornice and stepped out into a new world of blinding sunlight glinting on the snow and magnificent distant views. Quickly, we untied the rope and raced to the summit—to look out over half a dozen counties, from the cities to the sea and far beyond. And that is how I always think of Bowfell—a wonderful mountain to look out from, a shy pyramid full of quiet character.

Crinkle Crags

Another of the hills I can see from my study window is Crinkle Crags—a blue, knobbly ridge stretched across the sunset and ending abruptly with the north-east corner of Bowfell. But there's nothing smooth or ordinary about Crinkle Crags and it is the wrinkled shape of the mountain, so untypical of Lakeland, that we find so fascinating. If the bumps were a little sharper, I sometimes think, the sunset line would look not unlike a section of the Cuillin Ridge in Skye, but Crinkle Crags can never attract the fame of this imagined Scottish counterpart and, indeed, has difficulty even in getting into the guide-books.

When you come to think about it, this disregard of a fine peak is a little strange for there are only about twelve mountains in England higher than Crinkle Crags and no other mountain in

Lakeland with so many summits—five. While the ridge is as splendid a piece of rock architecture, with crags on either side, as you will find in the northern hills—excepting the major precipices—and provides tremendous scenery all round.

Few Lakeland ridge-walks are more impressive than this, although several may be comparable. All the way along this rooftree, perched between the sky and the valleys below, you are stepping on springy turf or firm rock ledges with easy stride, the invigorating air seeming to hurry you up and over the rises, with the wonderful feeling in your legs that you are covering great tracts of land at incredible speed. It is the rapidly changing views that provide the illusion—a different valley opening out below your feet every few minutes, the Langdale Pikes marching with you on your right, and, away to the left, the long line of the Scafells and the highest land in England.

And yet despite all this fine scenery and the undoubted exhilaration of the ridge a dozen guide-books either miss out the Crinkles altogether or dismiss them, with perhaps a one-line reference, as part of a route to Bowfell. An early work tells me: "Very wild and rough"—apparently as a deterrent rather than an invitation. While another warns that the walk should not be attempted in bad weather as compasses are liable to go wrong in this area. A much more accurate appraisal would be that Bowfell is one of the most splendid mountains in England, and perhaps the Queen of southern Lakeland, and that Crinkle Crags could be regarded as her consort, rather than her hand-maiden.

On Crinkle Crags, in fact, there are only a few places where minor compass deviations have been detected, and only when the traveller places his compass close to the ground. So, if you hold your compass in your hand or on your wrist and use it standing up, as most people do, it should work perfectly well all the way from Pike o' Blisco to Great End. Admittedly, people do sometimes find themselves on the wrong side of the ridge in bad weather—in Eskdale, perhaps, instead of in Langdale—not because their compass is playing tricks but simply because the ridge twists and turns so delightfully. You don't continue for long on a straight line on the Crinkles.

Among the greater glories of Crinkle Crags are the deep-cut ravines dipping down into the rugged recesses of Oxendale or the wild corries of upper Eskdale. These remote combes are among the best places in Lakeland for those seeking impressive, unspoiled scenery, and the agile will be able to scramble up to the ridge by way of any one of nearly a dozen routes, some

tracked but most of them unmarked. Often I've been up there
when the gullies have been filled with snow and the ridge has
only been reached by mountaineering approaching the serious.
One memory is of hacking through a snow-cornice after a bout
of step-cutting on the cold, shadowed side and then suddenly
stepping out on to the ridge into a blaze of sunshine, with snow
fields stretching away towards the sunset, and the whole ridge
a-glitter with silver and fire. But even with all the rock about,
there's no rock-climbing on the Crinkles, the crags proving, on
close acquaintance, either too loose or too easy and rarely yield-
ing worthwhile continuous routes. Across one or two of these
crags are curious terraces which may be traversed in safety,
provided one is not bombarded by stone falls initiated at the
summit. My dog once stuck on one of these ledges, but he can
be stupid when he feels like it. My children have scrambled
happily along them when they were only small youngsters.

Some of the finest tarns in Lakeland lie on or close to the
Crinkle Crags ridge. One popular approach to the summit rooftree is from the top of Wrynose Pass and on the way, underneath Cold Pike, will be found Red Tarn—one of several Red
Tarns in Lakeland—a quiet, shallow pool wherein dwell several
fat trout. And at the far end of the ridge, on the top of the col
that separates Bowfell from the Crinkles lie Three Tarns, with
one or two more tiny ones a short distance away. This little
cluster of tarns must be among the favourites of many who go
into the fells. Mostly, they are edged by weathered outcrops of
light, grey-coloured rock so that, in the sunshine, with plenty
of blue in the sky and reflections of the mountains in the water,
they make the perfect subject for the colour photographer or
painter.

There are only two very small tarns on the ridge itself,
although there are more on Shelter Crags which is really a con-
tinuation of the Crinkles and makes seven knobs in all. One of
the tarns lies quite close to the summit, the highest crinkle. Not
far away, only about thirty yards from the cairn, is a spring
trickling out from below a boulder—perhaps the nearest spring
to any summit in Lakeland. The view from the top of the
Crinkles is superb and embracing, although it includes nowadays
the cooling towers of the Calder Hall atomic-power station. A
much more impressive sight is the long view down Eskdale to
the sea and there is an even finer picture opening out down the
twelve miles stretch of Dunnerdale.

One of the best rounds in Lakeland for the short day is up

The Band and over Bowfell and the Crinkles, while a longer walk might include the Langdale Pikes and, at the other end, Pike o' Blisco and Cold Pike. During most of this longer walk you are moving along the Cumberland-Westmorland boundary, starting from the Three Shire Stone at the head of Wrynose and keeping on the boundary watershed all the way until you reach the boggy ground at the 'back' of the Langdales. Occasionally when I've been this way I've diverged a little from the boundary on Cold Pike and traversed along the delightful terrace of Gaitkins—the place of the little goats, I think it means—and on to Red How and Stonesty Pike. This is a wonderful little-visited area which also lends itself especially to photography. The rocky ledges make delightful foregrounds for pictures embracing a wide area of southern Lakeland and you may spend a day on these slopes and perhaps never meet a soul.

Crinkle Crags to many people belong to Langdale—the valley with the shapeliest mountains in Lakeland stretched all around. The photogenic Langdale Pikes stand on one side, and on the other is the wonderful switchback of Crinkle Crags—the mountain the old guide-book writers missed out.

High Raise

The mountain you might call Lakeland's shop window rises exactly at the apex of the blunt wedge that Westmorland drives into Cumberland and just tips the 2,500-feet contour. In some ways it is a rather undistinguished summit, but at least it has the distinction of being in the exact centre of Lakeland—if you are not to a thousand yards or so either way. And the view from its broad summit plateau is one of the most splendidly embracing in the district. They call the mountain High Raise although when I was a lad we knew it as High White Stones.

It has always seemed to me rather a pity that Wordsworth's spoked wheel, representing the Lake District, has not a better hub—something, for instance, like Bowfell—but High Raise certainly fits the bill better than dreary Armboth Fell which, it could be argued, is really the exactly central peak of Lakeland.

Since you could ride across the top of High Raise on a bicycle if you took the trouble to carry one up that far it could hardly be described as a dramatic summit and yet from the cairn or near it you can pick out, grouped around the horizon, almost every mountain of importance in Lakeland. And in between, on a clear day, you can see the Scottish coast and some of the Border hills, and away to the south-east, the Yorkshire fells, with flat-topped Ingleborough particularly prominent.

The late M. J. B. Baddeley who knew a good viewpoint if he saw one, considered High Raise provided "perhaps the most comprehensive and even the finest panoramic view in the Lake District", and suggested that from its summit you could have the best possible lesson in local geography. And I think he was right. Only to the south-south-east, where you look across to Morecambe Bay, is the skyline unbroken by mountains, so that if you stand by the big cairn and slowly shuffle round through 360 degrees you may be able to identify sixty or more of them, especially if you use your map and compass.

On a sunny summer's evening, with the westering sun casting long shadows across the turf and bringing out the colours in the survey column so that even this man-made intrusion becomes a thing of beauty, I find this great grassy plateau a rewarding place. You feel, when you are standing on High Raise, quite remote from the circle of mountains because the summit-ridge itself is about a mile long and nearly as broad with the fell almost surrounded by deep-cut valleys and its slopes plunging steeply downwards. It seems remarkable in such a relatively small mountain area as Lakeland that one can be at the centre of so many hills and yet so far removed from most of them.

You reach the summit quite fresh, since the approach is across almost level ground and the view can be enjoyed immediately without first sinking down from exhaustion. Lazily revolving, one identifies first, perhaps, Skiddaw and Blencathra to the north and then the Dodds and the long line of the Helvellyn range with Dollywaggon Pike and St. Sunday Crag peeping up behind. And then Fairfield, Harter Fell, Red Screes and a glimpse of the Pennines with the Yorkshire hills a little further south and, with your back to Skiddaw, the Coniston Fells straight ahead.

Slowly turning towards the west, after a glimpse in the foreground of the cone of Pike o' Stickle, there first comes the bold shape of Crinkle Crags and then Bowfell and the Scafells, the highest land in England, with Great End showing plainly as the final spur of that magnificent ridge. Due west lies Great Gable, looking especially impressive from this angle, and then Pillar and Glaramara and some of the Buttermere fells, with the dramatically sharp precipice of Honister Crag, and, between Melbreak and Robinson, perhaps a glimpse of the Irish Sea.

The Grasmoor fells lie to the north-west and then the graceful peak of Grisedale Pike and the crinkly fells around Borrowdale, and a peep at both Bassenthwaite and Derwentwater with the Solway Firth—and perhaps Criffel—behind. And, in the middle distance, the sparkling pools of Angle Tarn near Esk Hause, and Tarn at Leaves on Rosthwaite Fell and the deep trough of Langstrath down the slopes to the west.

High Raise, with its least interesting side in Cumberland and its finer features in Westmorland, is the highest point of the central group of fells that includes the Langdale Pikes, but has little in common with the steeply turreted peaks that over-look Langdale. These provide the most photogenic skyline in Lakeland but few people bother to take pictures of High Raise which has no characteristic shape and is merely the highest point of the plateau. You point your camera outwards from High Raise, not at it.

The Ordnance Survey still use the name High White Stones on some maps but this descriptive title should really be applied only to the stony summit area. There is also a Low White Stones a little nearer to Greenup Edge. The late Rev. H. H. Symonds gave a fanciful reason (with his tongue in his cheek) for this name. He wrote that a Mr. Sergeant whose name, he said, was commemorated in nearby Sergeant Man was a West-morland rent collector. He tried to force entry into the wilder county of Cumberland—the county boundary shows the way of it—but the rough men of Cumberland took up great white stones and drove him away. More accurately, Mr Symonds, in his rather flowery style, described the stroll along the top of High Raise as "the best central walk in Lakeland. . . . This is the hub of the wheel, the nodal point for a man looking into space; it is Apollo's central temple for the worshipper. . . ."

But while the top of High Raise is all view with no foreground to speak of and no excitements in the immediate surroundings, the walk to the plateau is interesting enough. You may go up from Grasmere, Borrowdale, Wythburn or Dungeon Ghyll, the first (and the longest) of these routes being probably the most rewarding. A pleasant circular day's walk—or half-a-day for the very fit—is to go up Helm Crag from Grasmere, continue along the Gibson Knott ridge into Far Easdale and carry on to High Raise from the Greenup Edge col. You then complete the circle by continuing over Sergeant Man and following the Blea Rigg ridge down to Blind Tarn Gill. In this way, you can look at Easdale and Codale tarns and also the tiny tarns on and near the plateau. If you do this walk in the opposite direction you will,

I think, get a better impression of the size of High Raise for as you thread your way up through the foothills to the east of the Langdale Pikes you discover how these impressive outliers are really only buttresses to the huge mass of High Raise which, although not a very high mountain, is quite an extensive one.

Where the mountain really starts and finishes is not easy to decide. Its western slopes certainly rise from Langstrath while the Far Easdale track contains the fell to the north and the Langdale Pikes form its southern edge. But I like to think that eastwards High Raise continues all the way down to Grasmere, first down to the ledges where lie Codale and Easdale tarns and then down Easdale itself to the meadows below Helm Crag. All this lovely country leads up High Raise although you may hardly see the mountain until you get there. Perhaps High Raise may be rather a plain, shy hill but when you get there you feel you've achieved something and when you look around you know it has been worth the effort.

Esk Pike

Esk Pike, the rather shy peak at the top of England's loneliest dale head, is the mountain the map-makers missed—until a few years ago. Although it is the tenth highest mountain in Lakeland, or thereabouts, it was not given the dignity of a name on the popular sheets of the Ordnance Survey until, I think, 1964 but had to be content with a dot in the centre of a ring contour, and the figure in feet of its quite impressive height—2,903. This is not, however, to suggest that the splendid men of the Ordnance Survey have been dilatory—I would hasten to defend them against most charges—but rather to underline the bashful nature of the mountain.

For nobody ever says: "We're going up Esk Pike today"—there are so many other good things close at hand. Hardly ever is the mountain deemed worthy of a separate expedition, for it is surrounded by such splendid neighbours—Bowfell, Great End and the Scafells—and so it suffers from, or rejoices in, scant attention, depending how one looks on these things.

And yet every Lake District walker and mountaineer, as well as many valley-bound tourists, knows the mountain well enough while Esk Hause which crosses the northern flanks of the peak is the best-known mountain pass in the National Park. People, indeed, go over Esk Pike every week—and perhaps every day in the summer—but only on their way to or from Bowfell or perhaps Great End, so that a worthy mountain has tended to become no more than an incident on an upland walk.

But now that the map-makers have identified Esk Pike perhaps the mountain may occasionally be deemed worthy of seeking out for its own sake for when you come to examine it on all sides you find it has some personality of its own. For example, the long rocky ridge of Yeastyrigg Crags is a feature of which any mountain could be proud while no other Lakeland mountain that I can think of carries on its shoulders twin passes like Esk Hause and Ore Gap—passes that have been taking the traveller through the hills since long before the days of recorded history.

Seen from the north Esk Pike is hardly even a feature on the ridge and this may have had something to do with the Ordnance Survey's earlier decision not to accord the peak the distinction of a separate name. At one time I've no doubt the mountain was regarded as a spur of Bowfell, despite the drop of several hundred feet to the red earth of Ore Gap, and it was not until 1870 that it was given its individual name—by a geologist named Ward who was working on a survey. So you might say that Esk Pike, although known as a mountain by the iron-smelters of olden days bringing the ore out of Eskdale and by the stone-axe makers of Langdale thousands of years ago, is barely a hundred years old.

But while the mountain lacks distinction when viewed from the north it comes into its own when seen from Eskdale and the south as the graceful climax to the long, hummocky watershed that lies between Lingcove Beck and the Esk. And it compresses its attractions into comparatively small compass for it is only a small mountain in area—perhaps three-quarters of a mile across its shoulders—despite its considerable height and its long ridge sweeping down into the wilds of upper Eskdale.

Ore Gap, the high pass between Esk Pike and Bowfell, is a romantic place and one of the oldest trade routes in Lakeland. It is said that Langstrath was once well-wooded but was cleared by the iron-smelters who brought their ore from Eskdale by way of this steep pass. There are several spellings of the name, including Ewer Gap and Ure Gap, but Ore Gap seems the more likely especially as there is a vein of hematite passing through and you can see the bright red soil in the track. The vein runs well down the Eskdale side but I don't think it has ever been mined, presumably because of the inaccessibility of the place. Postlethwaite, the authority on mining in the Lake District, wrote somewhere that the deposits could only be made to pay if an inclined railway down to Eskdale was built—and, fortunately for lovers of the hills, this has never happened and now never will.

Over the top of Esk Pike and down the other side of the ridge to Great End is the gap of Esk Hause and here many people who claim to know the Lakeland mountains well are at fault, and the map-makers right. For the pass most of us loosely refer to as 'Esk Hause' is not the real pass at all, but merely the highest point of the route between Wasdale and Langdale. Esk Hause—and the Ordnance Survey maps clearly show it—is the high gap between Esk Pike and Great End—a route not used nearly so much as the wrongly named 'Esk Hause', known to thousands, that runs at right-angles to the real hause. So that 'Esk Hause', the popular highway known to every visitor to the mountains of Lakeland and often described as the highest pass in the district, is wrongly named. The real Esk Hause is at least three hundred yards away, about one hundred feet higher and runs from Eskdale to Borrowdale, at right-angles to the well-marked track with the wall-shelter at its highest point. Many guide-books will tell you that 'Esk Hause' between Sty Head Tarn and Angle Tarn is the highest pass in Lakeland but this is not so. The real Esk Hause at 2,490 feet might be so described but this is hardly a pass in the popular meaning of the word and it would probably be true to say that the highest pass in regular use by the public is Sticks Pass (2,420 feet) between Thirlmere and Ullswater.

Indeed, the popular 'Esk Hause' has really no connection with the Esk at all and should have some other name but anybody who tried to alter it would get nowhere at all. For it's been 'Esk Hause' since the hills became known to the general public and nine out of ten people who have walked this way from Langdale to Wasdale believe they've been over Esk Hause, and would never be convinced they'd been mistaken. So that although the false 'Esk Hause' passes closer to the summit of Allen Crags than that of any other mountain I'm not really tempted to try to rename it Allen Hause. It doesn't sound right and I'd be shattering a lot of illusions. In any case, whenever I go this way I always say I've been over Esk Hause, for it would take far too long to explain it every time. Esk Hause, of course, is a notorious place for getting lost in mist and bad weather. People are always landing down in Eskdale or Langstrath when they're making for Wasdale or Borrowdale, or vice versa, and every year search teams are put to considerable trouble by people who should have shown a little more care. On the other hand I have heard of an experienced fell-walker making for Langdale who, stopping to light his pipe when the mist was down, turned his back into the wind, and finished up in Upper Eskdale.

One of the best ways up Esk Pike is to follow the infant Esk to the true hause, passing Cam Spout and Dow Crag—some of us know it better as Esk Buttress—on the way, and then down the long ridge to the bridge over the Lingcove Beck and so down to Brotherilkeld. On my last visit, however, I went up from Cockley Beck and through lonely Moasdale, making my way back over the Crinkles and down through Adam-a-Cove. One of the snags of fell-walking with a motor car is that you have to get back to your vehicle and often retrace much of your ground. But the long ridge of Yeastyrigg, Gait and Lang Crags makes a very pleasant descent and this is a part of Lakeland where you may never meet another soul, even in midsummer. All this is fine, rough, unspoiled country and the round of the fells that encircle the Esk can make a most enjoyable, although a long and rather tiring day.

As I have said, the summit of Esk Pike is not often visited because the track along the ridge goes a little to the left of the highest point and most people are either on their way to or coming away from Bowfell. It is, though, a fine viewpoint and a particularly magnificent grandstand for a sight of the Scafells, rising splendidly out of the depths of Eskdale.

Esk Pike lies entirely in Cumberland, but only half a mile outside the Westmorland boundary that encircles the head of Langdale. Perhaps it is a mountain we don't know really well— a mountain hidden among more exciting neighbours and not even named until a hundred years ago. But even so, a peak well worthy to stand at the head of Eskdale—that wild lonely dale-head that sees fewer visitors than the other central valleys of Lakeland and has remained more or less unchanged for something like a thousand years.

Helm Crag

Perhaps we shouldn't call Helm Crag—hardly 1,300 feet high— a mountain, but as it must be one of the best-known hills in the country we can't very well ignore it. Especially as it has more character and shape than many mountains twice its height and a graceful charm that, for me, seems to typify the peaceful loveliness of a Lakeland summer evening.

Unfortunately, however, to many people Helm Crag—they

may only know it as the hill on the right as they travel down
Dunmail Raise from Keswick—means only 'the Lion and the
Lamb', one of the popular tourist sights in Lakeland. For two
hundred years or more travellers going over the pass on horse-
back or in wagonette or motor coach have looked across at the
shapely fell, made sure they could pick out the lion and the
lamb, and then carried on their way, well satisfied. Few have
known the name of the fell and perhaps fewer still have cared.
All that mattered was that they should have the eyesight and the
imagination to spot what tens of thousands of others had seen
before them. What percentage of all these thousands have
bothered to scramble up the little hill and see the rocks from
close at hand I can't guess, but for a summit only half a mile
away from the main highway through Lakeland, Helm Crag is
surprisingly neglected.

It seems a pity that a grand little fell like Helm Crag should
be saddled to its fancied resemblance to animals and other
objects and regarded by the uninformed as little more than a
peep-show. For, with the necessary imagination, you can spot
many odd things on top. From somewhere near the top of
Dunmail Raise the summit rocks are said to resemble a huge
cannon or howitzer and from lower down the pass they become
an old woman seated at an organ. You are not necessarily looking at the same rocks in seeing the different figures and the issue
is further confused by there being two sets of the Lion and the
Lamb, as well as a Lion Couchant. I have never bothered to sort
it all out but Mr. Wainwright, the guide-book writer, says the
'official' Lion and the Lamb are formed by the rocks at the south-
east end of the summit ridge and are most effectively viewed
from the Swan Hotel in Grasmere. At the north-west end of the
ridge are the rocks forming the crouching lion (popularly 'The
Lion and the Lamb') as seen from half-way up the pass, or 'The
Howitzer' as seen from Dunmail Raise. They also provide
'The Old Lady at the Organ'.

But the summit of Helm Crag is a much more interesting
place than all this roadside fancy might lead one to expect. It is,
for example, one of the very few summits in the Lake District
only attainable by the use of the hands as well as the feet. The
actual summit is the top of the head of the (unofficial) lion or
howitzer, although the Ordnance Survey use the head of the
official lion, which is slightly lower. You scramble to the top of
Helm Crag up a sloping slab to reach an airy perch above a
wilderness of tumbled rock.

There is more rock and crag on top of modest little Helm Crag than on the summits of many of the bigger mountains of Lakeland. The summit ridge itself carries the strangely-shaped rocks you see from the road but there are also many other lumps of crag besides a moat-like depression and a rocky parapet high above the precipice of Raven Crag. Flowers grow in the rocky clefts, and in the shattered remains of what must have once been an impressive crag are many caves where a party could spend a comfortable night. Somewhere within this magnificent chaos of tumbled rocks that litters the curious trough just below the summit there is, I believe, a particularly fine inner cave where you could hide a fair company of people, but whenever I've gone exploring up there I've always found myself without a torch. And nearly always with my dog Sambo who *will* keep disappearing into awkward places, and constantly requires rescue. But some time I'll remember to take a torch, leave Sambo behind for once, and seek out the hidden chamber. Old Grasmere folk also tell me that the trough is really the crater of an extinct volcano, and that curious pear-shaped stones found near Blind Tarn, across the valley, had been hurled out as hot bubbles millions of years ago. You can trace the course of an old road, perhaps a Roman road, along the slope of the hill and down almost to the moraine heaps around Dunmail Raise.

The last time I was on Helm Crag was a sunny winter Sunday and I remember sitting up there and thinking how fortunate I was to be perched in such a delightful spot on such a perfect morning. There seemed to be nobody else on the hill and Sambo had gone off exploring on his own so that the peace and quietude was complete. The mists were still hanging in the meadows but above them the fells soared steeply towards blue skies. A cotton-wool haze lay over the waters of Windermere and the woodlands spiked through the greyness, but the fellsides sparkled in the sunlight and here and there a tarn or a mountain pool flashed silvery as a mirror. Perched on the head of 'The Lion' I could see and hear the cars going over Dunmail Raise, five hundred feet below—little toy cars in blue, yellow or grey, they seemed—and the pleasant sounds of pails rattling in a dairy or farm dogs at play came winging up the fellside on this stillest of winter mornings.

On the way up the fell I had disturbed the jackdaws in the little crag where the holly trees grow and for half an hour listened to the liquid call of a curlew mournfully circling the summit without spotting him. Sometimes I could just catch the murmur of a waterfall in the next valley but there was little else to hear and the fell country seemed deep in its winter sleep.

And Helm Crag is the perfect setting for a warm summer evening. From the summit there is often a wonderful sunset view and the vale of Easdale below is one of the most perfect places in Lakeland to reach at the end of a long day. There is a peaceful serenity about this little valley that has always captivated me, besides attracting many people of discernment to make their homes there. You can walk up Helm Crag in half an hour or so and continue easily along the ridge to Gibson Knott and Calf Crag, returning by way of Far Easdale—one of the most rewarding evening or half-day walks in the district. Or you can finish an Easdale walk by coming down the front of Helm Crag as the blue shadows slowly creep up the golden hillsides and the smoke rises quietly from the cottage chimneys. Soon the first lights will be appearing through the dusk in Grasmere, and another simple day in the hills comes to an end.

When the time comes when I have to give up rock-climbing and serious fell-walking—I hope it's a long time off yet—I like to think that I will still be able to get up Helm Crag to enjoy the scenery and the solitude, and perhaps watch the sunset creep down behind the Langdales.

5

THE HONISTER SKYLINE

(Around Buttermere)

High Stile

THERE is no finer summer's evening walk in Lakeland than that
along the smooth switchback of the Buttermere fells. Spread out
on all sides are sunlit or cloud-capped hills from Skiddaw to the
Scafells and from Gable to Helvellyn and, if the air is clear, you
will catch a glimpse of the Solway Firth and, far beyond, the
blue shapes of the Scottish mountains. Steep slopes and crags on
one side dip down to the unspoiled loveliness of Buttermere
while on the other hand is the deep trough of Ennerdale with
the bold precipice of Pillar Rock soaring high above the conifers.

Of the shapely triumvirate of High Crag, High Stile, and
Red Pike, High Stile is the central and highest peak and for me
has most charm. Its views are the most extensive, too, and
while it lacks Red Pike's steep sweep to Bleaberry Tarn, it is
most splendidly girt with crags and contains the wonderful
little hanging valley of Birkness Combe.

Sixty years ago W. G. Collingwood exactly caught the spirit
of Buttermere. He wrote: "I always think of this valley as made
by Heaven for summer evenings and summer mornings; green
floor and purple heights, with the sound of waters under the
sunset, or lit with the low north-eastern sun into pure colour
above, and the greyness of the dew upon the grass. . . ."

This is splendid writing and expresses much better than I
can manage my own feeling for this delectable valley which, on
the right day, has no equal for quiet beauty in England. And
Buttermere, for nearly as long as I can remember, has meant

High Stile and Birkness Combe; the stroll around the head of the lake and up into the hollow below the crags in the morning, with the sun on one's back; the long, happy days on warm, rough rock, and the trot down to the valley in the evenings, with the shadows lengthening across the close-cropped turf.

I must have been on High Stile many times in mist, rain and snow but my memories of this corner of Lakeland are nearly all of sunny days, for High Stile and his neighbours have always seemed friendly fells. Mostly, we've gone there in the summer time to climb on dry, warm rocks, because on Grey Crag in Birkness Combe you can be in the sunshine all day long and even go to sleep between pitches if you feel like it, which I've done more than once. Even on a wild day in winter, with a gale blowing across the ridge, you can sometimes climb in comfort on these clean, rough slabs and steep walls—well protected from the elements by their position, tucked just below the summit. And high up on these crags in summer time you can detect the sweet smell of the herbs far below on the corrie floor or lie in a rock recess on a couch of bilberries idly eating the purple fruit. Down in the combe the insects may be whirring in the scorched grass, the Herdwicks slowly seeking out the more succulent grazing between the boulders, and the becks sliding and trickling down the fellside.

There are few better places for a lone camper in the whole of Lakeland than in these lonely, rock-strewn corries and I know of a dozen patches of turf by the side of tinkling becks where you can sleep up there in perfect comfort and awake in the morning to the glory of a Lakeland dawn. And Collingwood's delightful description is the reward of the lone camper when he opens his tent flap on the slopes of High Stile on a summer morning, or takes his last look at the blue hills before turning in for the night.

These grey rocks of High Stile were only 'discovered' by the climbers less than sixty years ago but now have become a popular playground for both novices and experts. But thankfully, not *too* popular, for it is still a long walk up from the valley and this corner of Lakeland remains less spoiled than many others. As you take in the rope on these pleasant rock walls you look across at the ridge crossing the mountain to High Crag and, as often as not, may see walkers on the skyline, looking from this distance no more than moving matchsticks. Sometimes, too, walkers spot the climbers, but often, because of the shape of the fellside, they pass above them, unaware that not far below

Scafell Pike, Scafell and Pillar from High Stile

people are happily grappling with problems of verticality. Once, perched high up on one of these climbs I watched, throughout a long, hot afternoon, a cragfast sheep on a buttress on the opposite side of the combe. I saw it make repeated efforts to scramble up or down and finally, when we had decided we ought to abandon our climb and make our way across the valley to its rescue, we saw it slither all the way down to the foot of the crag. Possibly the approach of another rescue party—not seen by us— had frightened it into making the last desperate leap which had, surprisingly, brought it to safety. For it was quite unharmed after a broken fall of at least fifty feet.

High Stile is not a mountain of many features—just a rounded height on a noble ridge, encircled with crags, with a long shoulder sweeping down towards Buttermere and, on the other side, the steep drop towards the Liza and the conifers of Ennerdale. Few people walk to the top for the sake of the climb and nothing else, for High Stile is best used as part of the whole ridge or as a rock-climbing centre. So that the only tracks I know are those along the summit ridge and up through the combe to the crags. But few climbers who have spent the day on the crags can resist the walk along the ridge at the end, and the best days combine the two. The last time I was up there we carried on from our crag over the top of High Stile and Red Pike, and down by Scale Force although this meant a fair walk along the main road back to the car. It was airy walking, I remember, along the heights, passing in turn the saucer-shaped corries of Birkness, Bleaberry and Ling combes, with the turreted crags down on the right of the scalloped ridge and, on the left, in great contrast, the wooded fellside dropping into Ennerdale. And then beyond The Saddle the scene suddenly changed as the great Cumberland plain opened out ahead and a few minutes later we were among the roar and crash of Scale Force and then down through the meadows to the lake.

Red Pike is a fine mountain of character—red because of its pink Ennerdale granite—and seems almost to lean over Bleaberry Tarn and the lake of Buttermere far below. The fine cascade of Sourmilk Gill tumbles down from the tarn to the lake, and Scale Force, at the end of the ridge, is one of the best waterfalls in Lakeland. And at the other end of this noble ridge is the steep buttress of High Crag and, to make a longer day of the walk, across Scarth Gap, the wonderful, craggy upthrust of Haystacks, with its tarns and surprises round every corner. All this is splendid country for the young in heart and the grey

6

Dale Head crags from High Spy

rocks of High Stile make this mountain for me the queen of the Buttermere fells.

Robinson

Some people don't like Robinson as the name of a Lake District mountain, but for me the name has a friendly, familiar ring, and suggests stolidity—unimaginative, perhaps, but reliable. And Robinson the mountain is rather like that—maybe a dull hump, with nothing very spectacular about it, but a few special qualities hidden away if you care to seek them out.

Many, many mountains have been named after people. The Rockies are full of them and Everest itself was named after a map-maker, so there's nothing strange about such a name in the Lakeland fells, where we also have Harrison Stickle and John Bell's Banner. Perhaps Smith or Jones would have been an unfortunate name but I see nothing wrong with Robinson which is as good a local name as any. There are four columns of Robinsons in the Cumberland and Westmorland telephone directory, but fewer than fifty Braithwaites, which is a name bound up with the history of many parts of the two counties.

If the mountain had been named after John Wilson Robinson, the pioneer cragsman and statesman farmer who lived down in Lorton not ten miles away, perhaps nobody would have grumbled, for if ever there was a man of the mountains it was that cheerful personality. But Robinson the mountain was named long before men began to climb rocks for fun, and one authority states the name dates from a certain Richard Robinson who bought the mountain as part of an estate centuries ago. For years they called it Robinson's Fell but all my guide-books, except the very oldest, refer to it—if they mention the mountain at all—simply as Robinson.

My oldest guide-book—a 1799 edition of Thomas West— describes Robinson but does not name the mountain. West wrote: "In approaching the head of Newlands Hause, on the left, a mountain of purple-coloured rock presents a thousand gaping chasms, excavated by torrents that fall into a basin, formed in the bosom of the mountain, and from thence precipita- ting themselves over a wall of rock, become a brook below.

"In front is a vast rocky mountain, the barrier of the dell, that opposes itself to all further access. Among the variety of water- falls that distinguish this awful boundary of rock, one catches the eye at a distance that exceeds the boasted Lodore in height of rock and unity of fall, whilst the beholder is free from all anxiety of mind in the approach. Not one pebble or grain of sand offends; but all is nature in her sweetest trim of verdant turf, spread out to please her votaries."

This may sound a rather fanciful description of Moss Force which drops down to the Hause from the northern slopes of Robinson, but West had managed to hit on one of the features of the mountain—its waterfalls. For there are other pleasant cascades down Goat Crag on the Buttermere side of the mountain, and a whole series of splendid cataracts in Little Dale, between Robinson and its close neighbour Hindscarth.

There is also another quoted derivation of the name Robinson, which is that the mountain was originally called Robecon at the time of the Normans, and was used as a look-out station. Which of the two is right, I can't say, but I prefer to think that it was called after the man who bought the mountain. Perhaps it doesn't really matter, but Dick Robinson's fell sounds convincing enough for me and he was probably more local than the Normans.

Few people, I suppose, go up Robinson without continuing the walk to Dale Head for the mountain is more of a feature on a ridge than a hill to be ascended for its own sake. But this particular ridge-walk is one of the finest in the district—an airy tightrope with splendid distant views, especially of Pillar and the Wasdale fells.

Seen from Buttermere, Robinson is rather disappointing—a bulky, uninteresting slope, with its summit tucked away out of sight, although the Goat Crag area, opposite Hassness, with its steep ravines and slabby rock, is quite impressive. I took my son, when he was a small boy, for one of his first climbs on these rocks but it was not a particularly successful initiation for the crag is hardly suitable for a beginner and lacks continuity for the expert.

Robinson is seen at its best from Newlands when its distinctive skyline gives it the appearance of straddling the head of the dale with strength and dignity. And from the Keswick area, when the sun is setting in the west, the mountain sometimes stands out most impressively, as it throws its long shadow down the valley. Probably the mountain's most impressive feature is the long ridge that sweeps down to Newlands flanked by the fine precipice of Robinson Crags. This is a fast way off the mountain and some of the earlier holders of the Lakeland twenty-four hours fell record came down this way and continued at the trot to the finish at Keswick. But during the more recent attempts on the record Robinson has merely been an incident in the long course. Several times I've sat near the top of Newlands Hause waiting for the tiny figures to top the summit on their way from Dale Head, and then, a few minutes later, we've watched them tripping down the zigzags to the right of Moss Force.

For the lazy walker who wants to bag an easy summit here's the opportunity—Robinson from Newlands Hause, involving only about fourteen hundred feet of ascent. And Dale Head from the top of Honister is even easier. But most people go up Robinson by way of Buttermere Moss—a long, rather dull trudge, with the Moss a nasty place in wet weather. This route follows the old peat-gathering track up the fellside, and I believe the track, graded for ponies, was first built of stones and then covered with turf. But nobody bothers to cut peat for fuel on the Moss nowadays. There are one or two tiny tarns on the Moss— the only ones on the mountain unless you include the old reservoir, originally built for the mines, in Little Dale on the north-eastern side of the fell.

The view from the summit of Robinson, provided you walk about a bit, is extensive and rewarding, one curious feature being that the top of Scafell Pike is almost exactly hidden by Great Gable. I write 'almost' advisedly because when I once referred to this point in an article several readers wrote in to say that if a good pair of field-glasses were used a thin segment of the top of the Pike could just be seen. And somebody else sought to prove by mathematics that the top few feet of the Pike should just be visible. All this may be true, although to me Great Gable seems to block the view completely. Perhaps I've never looked across on the right sort of day but it just shows how careful we writers have to be.

For me Robinson is an evening mountain—a mountain that can look well when sharpened and sculptured by evening shadows, and a mountain that often marks the end of a long day in the hills. And I still like the name—no matter who thought it up.

Dale Head

Dale Head is a friendly, honest mountain—a shapely, uncomplicated pyramid on the edge of a fine ridge, with steep crags where you might expect to find them, and an accommodating wire-fence running up towards the summit. Even its name is straightforward and accurately descriptive, unlike that of its near and bulkier neighbour, Robinson.

Few, if any, mountains in the Lake District are easier to ascend, if the walker is not ashamed to motor to the top of Honister Pass. True, Red Screes, for instance, is only a thousand feet or so above the populous summit of Kirkstone Pass, but nothing like so easy to reach as the top of Dale Head which may be attained by a 1,300-feet rise by easy pedestrianism with the fence to pull on, if desired. You can easily get up and down in an hour and the average agile youngster should be able to run the whole of the return journey without stopping.

But although Dale Head can be such an easy summit—I once met a man up there in city suit and shoes with a neatly rolled umbrella—it is, for several reasons, a very worthwhile mountain. For instance, it is the culminating point of one of the finest ridge walks in the district—Cat Bells, Maiden Moor, Eel Crags (or High Spy), Dale Head, Hindscarth and Robinson—and it sports on its shoulders steep, little-visited crags where the climber may select superb routes with little risk of having to take his place in the queue.

Most of all, however, the summit of Dale Head is a remarkably fine viewpoint—one of the best and most embracing in Lakeland—and is the unchallenged guardian of the Vale of Newlands, a dale of almost idyllic beauty. Ignore for a moment the southern view of the highest land in England and think of the superb view to the north—the view that bursts upon you quite suddenly the moment you reach the cairn. One moment you are treading the rather dull final slope to the north with nothing much ahead worth bothering about; then, suddenly, the ground drops away, the Derwent Fells, with old man Skiddaw at the back, rise up to greet you, and the whole of the green, hollowed Vale of Newlands lies smiling in the sunshine two thousand feet below your feet.

Six miles away—if you have chosen the right day—the sun glints on the rooftops of Keswick, looking like a toy village under the painted backcloth of Skiddaw and, far beyond the furthest Lakeland fells, you can pick out the Scottish hills. One end of Bassenthwaite Lake can just be seen beyond the Lorton Fells although the glories of Borrowdale are hidden behind the ramparts of Maiden Moor and Eel Crags. Directly in front of you, if the sun is favourable, the long ridge leading to the summit of Grasmoor stands up steep and sharp like a piece of stage scenery. The slopes of Causey Pike, Sail, Wandope and the rest appear quite vertical and the ridge itself, a pleasant but insect-ridden ridge in summer, can look, under snow, like a line of Alpine towers. Grisedale Pike peeps up behind this ridge and to your left the fells sweep round to the twin buttresses of Hindscarth and Robinson.

But it is the view immediately below your feet that is particularly entrancing. The ground appears to drop vertically down the contours to Newlands Beck which flows due north through a green, shadowed trough, scooped out with perfect symmetry. Three or four miles away farmsteads may be seen nestling among the trees, and if you are lucky you will see no movement whatever in the whole of the vast landscape below, except the quietly grazing sheep, and hear no sound. The perfect, pastoral scene.

And it is because the scene is so unspoiled, so peaceful, that we find it difficult to imagine the picture, three or four hundred years ago, when the valley housed an important industry and, the German miners were hard at work, tearing the minerals out of the ground. You can trace where some of the old workings used to run and see the zigzag tracks taken by the miners centuries ago when you are taking in the rope on the climbs on Eel Crags, but there is little sign of this long-forgotten industry to be seen on the ground and nothing at all from the summit of Dale Head. In Dale Head Mine itself, right underneath the summit on the north face of the mountain, was found copper ore, pyrites and malachite, and you can see the bright green veins of the metal in the spoil-heaps. But the sheds, water-wheels, crushing plants, furnaces and rubbish tips where they mined for led,a copper and silver have almost disappeared—swallowed up and covered over by kindly Nature. As I write, in 1967, there is some talk of their reopening the mines but whether anything will come of the project I cannot say.

But if you turn your back on this lovely view you can see in the foreground the scarred face of Honister Crag on Fleetwith where, for generations, men hanging in chains or working in dizzy galleries tore the rich, green slate out of the precipice. In more recent years they have worked on the southern flank of Dale Head itself so that both sides of the pass are pockmarked by crowbars and explosives. But hardly offensively so, for we may still marvel at man's ingenuity at winning wealth from these wild places, and admire the skills that make up an ancient and honourable local industry. And beyond Fleetwith on a clear evening you can see the Scafells, Pillar, Gable and the rest and sweep your eyes across most of Lakeland.

Surprisingly on so innocuous a mountain, I once spent an anxious hour or two on Dale Head. Two of us had walked from the top of Honister over Fleetwith, Haystacks, High Crag, High Stile, Red Pike down to Buttermere and then up again to Robinson but just below the summit my friend complained of cramp and wanted to rest for half an hour. He insisted, however, that I went on—I expected him to catch me up later when he had unknotted his leg muscles—so I carried on over Robinson and Hindscarth to the Dale Head cairn where I went to sleep in the afternoon sunshine. When I awoke, evening was approaching but there was no sign of my friend and I went back all the way to Robinson to look for him, without success. What had happened? Had he slipped down one of the gullies along the ridge and was now lying injured among the crags? I hurried back to Dale Head, shouting and peering down all the possible places, and then, getting thoroughly alarmed, decided to run down to Honister to raise the alarm. It seemed a long way, although I ran every yard of it, and I was very hot and exhausted as I approached the pass, only to see my friend climb out of the car and start slowly up the fellside towards Dale Head. We met and I'm afraid—after my initial feeling of relief—roundly abused one another. He was on his way to look for *me*, having descended direct to the head of the pass from Robinson. While I had been combing the crags on the ridge for him, he had been imagining me lying mangled at the foot of some gully and after an hour in the car, casting aside these morbid thoughts, had decided to do something about it. For the following quarter of an hour, I regret to say each remained ominously silent, thinking the most uncharitable thoughts about the other. Incidentally, the cairn where I went to sleep was wrecked years later by hooligans— just as the summit cairns on Pike o' Blisco, Lingmell and other tops have been pulled down by vandals. The Dale Head cairn has since been rebuilt but these madmen are still about in the fells, and nothing seems safe from their childish destruction.

The crags of Dale Head carry some of the finest and most difficult rock routes in the district, three climbs in particular on Buckstone How, south of the summit—Sinister Grooves, Groove Two and Buckstone Girdle—being in the 'very severe' category, as is also Dale Head Pillar on the north side of the mountain facing down Newlands. And there are other magnificent but less difficult routes for the average performer, some of them easily attainable from the quarry track that slants up the fellside from the top of the pass.

Dale Head has its own beautiful tarn on the shoulder east of the summit, a fine ravine just below the mine, and waterfalls just around the corner. The tarn, with an old sheep-fold close by, is a lovely place on a summer evening. Here you can lie, watching the outflow tumbling down through the reeds to the waterfalls of Newlands Beck far below, and be alone with your thoughts. The walk along the ridge to Hindscarth, with its scooped corries on your right hand is a delight, and the tramp down Newlands to Little Town and Stair, as the sun goes to rest behind the Derwent Fells, makes the perfect ending to a day in the Lakeland fells.

Fleetwith Pike

Perhaps the most impressive scene from any main road in Lakeland—the nearest thing in England to the grandeur of the descent into Glencoe—is the dramatic view that greets the traveller when he reaches the top of Honister Pass and looks down towards Buttermere. Preferably, for maximum effect, he should see it on a wild, stormy day—the huge black mass of Honister Crag soaring up to the vertical on his left, the mountain wall of Dale Head, Hindscarth and Robinson to the right and, straight ahead, the steep winding descent through the gorge towards the lakes and the Buttermere meadows, the beck noisily tumbling down beside the road, and the valley floor littered with the great boulders that have crashed down from the crags.

"One of Britain's most impressive scenes," was how an early writer described the view and many people will agree with him for in few other places in this country can the ordinary main road traveller get so close to mountain savagery of this order.

The scene assumes its dramatic quality largely because of Honister Crag—a thousand feet of vertical precipice, tilted slabs and splintered screes, apparently impregnable and, to those un-accustomed to such splendid architecture, grim, foreboding and even frightening. Nearly all the great crags of Lakeland—Pillar Rock, Scafell Crag, Dow Crag, Gable Crag, Dove Crag, Bowfell Buttress and many more—are tucked away out of sight, at close hand, of the ordinary tourist, but here is a splendid precipice rising just in front of their noses. And the crag becomes even more interesting to many visitors when it is explained to them that the great wall is really a quarry—a place where men go to work every day, hacking out the rock from the very bowels of the precipice to make the best roofing slates in the world. Or you can thrill the incredulous visitor even further by pointing out the galleries across the face down which the quarrymen used to drag their sledges filled with the shattered rock or, show them, high up, where the wall tilts towards the vertical, where men used to hang out on ropes and chains, splitting the rock and prizing it out in great chunks. It was exciting, dangerous work for the very toughest breed of men and a story of ingenuity, skill and sometimes heroism that goes back for more than two hundred years.

Less than a hundred years ago the quarrymen were sleeping in small huts near the crag, only going home from the Saturday night to the Monday morning. Towards the end of last century the quarrymen would leave their provision lists at Teddy May's grocer's shop in Rosthwaite on the Saturdays, and the groceries for the week would be sent up to the quarries on the Monday mornings by Tom Braggs, who was carting the quarry slate at that time. It is said that Tom had one horse 'Old Dick' who could always be relied upon to take his master, dropped in the cart, safely home, if the carter had had 'one over the eight' in the Keswick pubs. Many of the quarrymen were extraordinarily strong and it was said of one Joseph Clark, of Stonethwaite, that he brought down the face of the crag in seventeen journeys no fewer than forty-two loads one day, moving nearly 11,000 pounds of slate. These journeys down the sloping galleries, with every muscle strained taut, required both nerve and strength and when they had deposited their loads at the bottom they climbed up the crag again, with their sleds, heavy sleds of oak and iron, on their backs. In Wordsworth's time the men used to hang out on the cliff in frail basket chairs or in a rope seat, drilling holes in the vertical rock so that big slabs might be dislodged by gunpowder. Today most of the work is done inside the mountain and machinery used to an increasing extent.

Certainly, the quarrymen have altered the shape of Fleetwith Pike, or at least its north side, but their activities have never spoiled the scene for me. There has always seemed a particular fascination about the daring and enterprise of the men who carved up this great crag, but the cliff still seems unbowed and will remain so even if gouged out for another thousand years. While the men, although dwarfed by the size of the scenery, remain proud and determined.

Nature seems to have put things into a proper perspective at Honister Crag even though she is fighting a losing battle on the pass. For Honister Pass is a sorry sight on a sunny, summer Sunday nowadays. Gone completely is the feeling of quiet majesty and awe-inspiring solitude and in its place is a long procession of noisy, smelly vehicles, nose to tail, stretched out over the pass, picnic parties every few yards down the slopes into Buttermere, and jostling crowds on the summit. Traffic and crowds have done more damage to the amenities of this wild pass than generations of hacking and hewing by the quarrymen.

Not very long ago 'The Honister Round', one of the last of the horse-drawn coach-tours in Lakeland, went over the pass—"the finest drive," they said, "in Britain." The coaches left Keswick at ten o'clock in the morning, went by way of Lodore and Rosthwaite, over the pass and down to Buttermere and then back over Newlands Hause to Keswick. You were back in Keswick at six o'clock, and the cost fifty years ago was six shillings for the day.

But the fine road over Honister yields many easy ways into the mountains. Even quite elderly walkers find they can ascend to the Drum House, just south of Fleetwith summit, and then continue along the well-graded Moses' Sledgate towards Wasdale. This fine track through the fells is supposed to have been planned by Moses Rigg who worked the green slate in Honister Crag and also at Dubs Quarry at the 'back' of Fleetwith Pike. He may also have done a big trade in smuggling wad or plumbago taken from the mine in Borrowdale and the ruined hut on Gable Crag might have been one of his hideouts. Nowadays the ruined quarry hut at Dubs Quarry has been converted into comfortable headquarters by the Keswick Mountaineering Club and is one of the highest situated climbing huts in the Lakeland fells.

But there is more to Fleetwith Pike than the precipice of Honister Crag and the story of the quarries. The summit, for example, provides a remarkable view of Buttermere and the three lakes and away to the Solway, and looking south from Criffel in the Scottish Lowlands and perhaps—although I've not checked on this—from The Merrick, Fleetwith Pike is often the first Lakeland peak to be recognized. The descent of the mountain down the long ridge into Buttermere, with splendid views ahead all the way, is airy but easy, although it was the scene of a fatal accident in 1887. A woman was coming down the ridge and at one point held her alpenstock straight in front of her. The point stuck in the ground, she slipped, her chin caught on the butt of the stick, and in the fall her neck was dislocated. A white cross, with the legend "In the midst of life we are in death" carved upon it, was erected at the spot and still serves as a reminder that you can never be too careful in the hills.

There is also a route down the face of Honister Crag for the more athletic but the crag has no attraction for rock-climbers, although there are some fine routes on the crags on the opposite side of the pass. But Fleetwith Pike *does* yield some climbing, all of it round the 'back' of the mountain in Warnscale. This is one of the least-visited corners of central Lakeland—a quiet, rather brooding place in stark contrast to the clamour of the pass, with a track zigzagging up the combe to the tumbled wilderness between Fleetwith Pike and the Haystacks. Fleetwith is protected by crag to the north and to the west, and on this western wall will be found Striddle Crag, with several worthwhile climbing routes and some very fine and unusual situations. This is a place to visit on a Bank Holiday when all the better known haunts are crowded with people. Here you will find another world, a place of delightful pools and waterfalls, rounded crags, peaty hollows and clean sunny rocks for climbing. So don't condemn Fleetwith Pike as just a quarried precipice, for the mountain has another side, and on a hot day Warnscale Bottom, with its splashing beck and the murmurings of sheep, may be the paradise you are seeking.

6

FAIRFIELD AND HIS FRIENDS

(East of Dunmail)

Fairfield

THE surging sweep of uplifted land that cuts off Ambleside's view to the north is the delightfully, although inaccurately-named Fairfield—one of the popular mountains of Lakeland but, paradoxically, one of the least-known. For Fairfield, a two-faced mountain if ever there was one, is mostly known as the culminating feature of one of the favourite 'horseshoe' rounds of the district—a pleasant but rather dull mountain of grass, with little to commend it except its bulk and height and its value as a viewpoint. Whereas, in fact, Fairfield is a craggy and quite complicated mountain of character, the highest mountain after Helvellyn and its satellites, to the east of the main highway through the National Park and, by any estimate, one of the principal mountains in Lakeland.

The reasons for the popular misjudgment of Fairfield are that nine-tenths of its visitors know it only from the south and that its magnificent northern face looks out over the, fortunately, still 'undiscovered' valley of Deepdale. Several years ago when I was assisting in the compilation of a rock-climbing guide two of us went into Deepdale to climb and measure the routes on dozens of occasions, and I can't remember ever seeing anybody else in the valley. Indeed, many people—some of them quite well-used to the district—have never even heard of Deepdale—except as the headquarters of a football club. But, in fact, Deepdale is one of the best valleys in Lakeland—secluded, ringed by fine crags, almost untracked, and the home of the

finest of our mountain birds. No signpost points into the valley
and it is still unlittered by orange peel and sandwich wrappings.
And the 'real' side of Fairfield dominates this lonely dale—the
side that makes the mountain one of my favourites.

It is a strange thing that the popular, grassy, relatively
featureless—from its southern side—mountain should have become, to some of us, an important rock-climbing area, and
perhaps even more strange that this aspect of its value should
have been unknown twenty years ago. Although Deepdale has
been known to the discerning for generations, and although the
crags of Fairfield have always been admired from Dollywaggon
and elsewhere by people who look for these things, it was not
until 1948 that Alfred Gregory, the Everest mountaineer, made
the first route on these crags and another four years after that
before a wave of exploration swept up these lonely rock faces.
But today the two main coves which contain the principal crags
provide some of the longest and hardest climbing routes in
eastern Lakeland and, because of their exposure, lack of shelter,
steepness and greasiness in bad weather, several of these climbs
have about them a mountaineering quality not readily found in
this part of the world. There are a few easy climbs here, but
most of them are serious undertakings, so that, by and large,
Fairfield, the nice grassy mountain is, on its northern face, a
place only for the expert.

You can look down into the main coves of Fairfield that give
the mountain its character from its broad summit which, because
of its plateau-like shape and its over-profusion of cairns, is an
easy place on which to get lost in bad weather. One Easter,
several years ago, two girls walking over the summit missed
their way in a snow-storm and fell over one of the crags to their
death, and their bodies were not discovered until the snows
melted, despite one of the biggest searches ever organized up to
that time. Link Cove is the combe between Hart Crag and Fairfield, and Scrubby Crag lies high up in the cove, just below the
the tourists' path along the ridge. These very steep cracks and
chimneys provide many difficult climbs, and, lower down the
cove, there is Ern Nest Crag, once incorrectly styled Earnest
Crag on the Ordnance Survey sheet, but really taking its name
from the ern, or eagle, which used to frequent these wild precipices. The next main cove is Sleet Cove, closer under the summit of Fairfield, and containing the redoubtable Hutaple Crag
and Black Buttress, and separated from Link Cove by the fine
crags of Greenhow End, sometimes loosely called 'The Step'.

There are also other crags scattered around the coves and, at the very head of the dale, the splintered rocks of Cofa Pike, while even on the popular, southern side of the mountain there are the rocks of Black Crag and the little-visited wilderness of Calf Cove. So that walkers passing across the well-trodden summit should remember that climbers may be engaged on the steep northern and eastern cliffs below them and should take care not to send rocks dropping down on to their heads. I was once just in time to stop one thoughtless youngster from pushing a boulder over the edge of one of the crags which contains many severe routes. And walkers across the plateau are recommended to turn their eyes from the admittedly wonderful prospect and admire the sculptured north face of the mountain, as seen eastwards from the summit, or, better still, from the top of Cofa Pike or from Deepdale Hause. They may see, in particular, a curiously shaped gully, bent into the shape of a bow. This is Curving Gully, nearly five hundred feet high, one of the easier climbs in the amphitheatre, but a fine route which used to be full of loose rock but is now much safer. There are harder climbs further to the east and on an earlier ascent of one of these I remember once starting to pull up on a hold which caused a huge mass of rock to tilt out slowly. Fortunately my second, who was perched only a few feet away, was able to come to my assistance, and we were able to shout to the third man on the screes to take cover before the block, which must have weighed several hundredweights, crashed down to the foot of the crag. The climb is now much more difficult.

This, then, is the main glory of Fairfield—its magnificent northern face and the seclusion of lovely Deepdale—and, for the rest, there is the fine summit view, the splendour of the 'Horseshoe' round over Hart Crag and Dove Crag starting and finishing at Rydal, especially if this is done on a sunny, winter's day, and the sheer bulk and impressiveness of the mountain wall. Deepdale is incomparably the finest approach, but Rydal Head is also a wonderful place. It is circumnavigated by hundreds every summer but few people bother to go down into the combe. The mountain has no tarn of its own, but the waters of Grisedale Tarn, where Wordsworth in 1800 parted with his brother John, later drowned at sea, lap the skirts of its western slopes. To Harriet Martineau "dear old Fairfield" was her favourite mountain and many people may agree with her. Certainly Fairfield, the real Fairfield, is a mountain of character, a trap for the unwary, a testing ground for the agile, a grim peak in winter, and the lord of a cluster of lesser fells. There are few finer hills in Westmorland.

Dove Crag

Dove Crag, the black, overhanging precipice that looks down to Brotherswater from the heel of the Fairfield 'Horseshoe' is described in the climbing guide to the area, and rightly so, as "one of the most impressive cliffs in England". You can see it, high up over to the right from the foot of Kirkstone Pass as you approach its northern side and it will almost always be in the shadow, for Dove Crag faces the north-east and rarely catches the sun.

Its gentle name belies the true character of Dove Crag, which must be one of the steepest and most savage places in Lakeland. Much of the crag is overhanging and the rest either vertical or nearly so, while the screes below are among the most precipitous and shattered in the district. Indeed, I have heard it said that the cove at the foot of the crag was once a crater of a volcano.

The crag gives its name to the mountain on which it stands and no doubt takes its name from Dovedale, which is one of the loveliest and least-spoiled corners in the National Park. This little glen which winds eastwards down to Hartsop Hall has lush green meadows and lazy beds of shingle at its foot, cool hazel woods and splashes of juniper higher up, waterfalls and glorious rock pools and, at its head, a wild tangle of steep cliffs and dark hollows. Apart from the ruins of an old lead-mine near the entrance to the dale the valley carries little evidence of the hand of man. But I am forgetting the other ruin almost underneath the crag—the remains of a stone hut where, I've heard, members of some religious sect, to escape persecution, used to hold their meetings perhaps a couple of hundred years ago. To reach it demands some effort for it is at least an hour away from the nearest habitation, but no doubt—if the story is true—the worshippers thought the toil worthwhile.

I've been on the mountain many times, sometimes walking over its crest and sometimes climbing on the crag itself. One occasion, by a macabre coincidence, was the day before a young undergraduate fell to his death on the crag one July. This is the only fatal accident that I can remember on this steepest of crags. It was a perfect day for our visit, hot and sunny in the dale with just enough breeze on the tops to keep the flies away, and

splendid views, only slightly marred by heat-haze. You can't
drive into Dovedale nowadays—unless you are on business—as
you used to be able to do, and so the entrance to the dale has
avoided being turned into a car-park, the penalty suffered by
other lovely places. There were four of us and the dog and we
took our time, preferring at first the delights of the beck to
more energetic exercise higher up the fell. The cattle were
wading in the shallows by the meadows and it was too hot for
Sambo to be interested in the sheep. We inspected the woods to
see what the October nut harvest might be like and, further up
the fellside, lay down on scented banks of thyme for a smoke or
to wash down chocolate and raisins with ice-cold water from the
beck. Tiny insects whirred in the bracken and the only other
sound, apart from the splashing of the beck, was the distant
shrill of aircraft making vapour patterns across the sky.

Approaching the rough country at the foot of the crag we
heard voices and eventually espied two climbers high up among
the overhangs—or rather the feet of one of them and an occasional arm or leg of the other with, now and again, a flicker of
rope in between, for they were mostly hidden by the great bulge
of the face. The sight took me back to a day, several years
before, when I managed to get up Hangover, most appro-
priately named and at that time the hardest climb on the crag,
and one of the most forbidding in the district. But I couldn't
look at it nowadays and I've no doubt would have difficulty in
getting off the ground on some of the even harder routes that
have since been put up on the crag. These two climbers were on
one of the new routes and I wished them well, but we were
bound for something very much easier. I remember these were
the only two people we saw all day until we got back to
Brotherswater.

The old hut was still there but even more tumble-down than
on previous visits. We also inspected some of the shelters among
the rocks where, if you are so inclined, you can spend a fairly
comfortable night amid most dramatic scenery and be on the
spot for your rock-climbing the next morning. A friend of mine
once left a stove, fuel and tinned-food in one of these rock
shelters in preparation for a night out on some future weekend but when we went up there, several weeks or months later,
he found his cache had been rifled. I don't think this sort of thing
would have happened before the war. But we weren't planning a
night out this lovely July day but merely some gentle exercise.
So leaving our wives to sunbathe by the beck and the dog to

Honister Crag on Fleetwith Pike

sleep in the shade of a rock, we turned our faces to the crag which we finally surmounted by a modest route befitting our age and lack of form.

Dove Crag is topped by a wall, presumably to prevent sheep from tumbling over the overhangs, but if you are exploring downwards from the summit you need to get below this wall to savour the drop. Nervous walkers should keep away but if you have a good head for heights you can work downwards until you reach a place above the overhang. Here, by lying flat on your stomach, you can drop a stone straight on to the screes, perhaps three hundred feet below. The first route on the crag was climbed in 1910 by Lieut-Col. H. Westmorland of Threlkeld. He recalls that on the way up a steeply tilted slab on which he was perched "slid gently outwards about four inches with me clinging to it". It must have been a nasty moment but there was no further movement and in a second or two he was able to step gingerly upwards and then pull himself over a little overhang on to a safe ledge. The main feature of the crag as seen from Dovedale is a 300-feet hanging gully that splits the cliff in two. This is Inaccessible Gully—so called before it was climbed, by combined tactics, in 1937—while Hangover, which picks its way through the central overhangs, came two years later.

Near the top of Dove Crag is a natural cave from which a remarkable view of Dovedale and Patterdale may be obtained as from a window and there are also some interesting rock formations in this area. The mountain itself is a fell of sharp contrasts. To the east there is the main crag and several minor crags, as rough and rocky a fellside as anywhere in Lakeland, but elsewhere the mountain falls in long grassy slopes or is joined by smooth depressions to other heights in the Fairfield 'Horseshoe'. For this reason many walkers doing the 'Horseshoe' round from Ambleside pass over Dove Crag, the mountain, without realizing that a few hundred yards away to the north-east from the broad summit plateau and its crumbling stone wall is the tremendous precipice that gives the featureless summit its name.

Dove Crag has its own little tarn, just to the north of the main precipice, but much more rewarding are the pools and waterfalls in Dovedale Beck and in Hogget Gill, the fine rocky gorge overlooked by Stand Crags and the knobbly feature known as The Stangs. Hogget Gill is a perfect gem—just a little over a mile away from the traffic on Kirkstone Pass—and an excellent

7

St. Sunday Crag from Gough Memorial on Helvellyn

alternative descent route from the mountain. Due north, on the far side of the main beck are the prominent slabs of Gill Crag, formerly known as Dovedale Slabs—one of the best places in Lakeland, I used to think, for learning the craft of rock-climbing in nailed boots.

Back down at Brotherswater after a visit to Dove Crag the precipice nearly always appears menacing and gloomy and especially in winter time. For the snows cling to the surrounding fells but leave the black face of the crag untouched so that it stands out sharply, the only dark mass in a white world. This is the Dove Crag I prefer to remember—the cliff rather than the mountain.

St. Sunday Crag

Somewhere in an old guide-book, published more than fifty years ago, I remember reading: "St. Sunday Crag is *the* Ullswater mountain," and, when you come to think about it, it's not a bad description. For St. Sunday Crag dominates the western reach of Ullswater far more dramatically than Helvellyn and, in a sense, commands the whole length of the lake better than any other mountain. And yet its summit is disappointing and the mountain not especially popular. Not many people bother with the ascent for its own sake, but are more likely to use the mountain as a pleasant route off Fairfield. Which is very strange, for St. Sunday Crag is a massive, soaring fell, one of the steepest in Lakeland, with a fine shape when seen from any angle.

Who St. Sunday was I've little idea. W. G. Collingwood suggested the name might be derived from St. Sanctum, but this doesn't help a great deal. I have also been told the name is thought to be derived from St. Dominic—the Saint of the Lord's Day—which suggests there might be some tradition of a religious house of this order in the district, but I have no facts to substantiate this. There is a St. Sunday's Beck to the south-east of Kendal, but no apparent connection between the two, and the old books named the mountain St. Sunday's Crag. But perhaps the name doesn't matter very much and it trips readily off the tongue, although it is really surprising how few people know the mountain. I was there one October climbing some of the new routes on the crag but when I happened to mention this a few days later to a friend who has been walking the fells for years he confessed he had never been on the mountain and had never even noticed the crag. And yet the Grisedale face of the mountain which drops nearly two thousand feet in half a mile is one of the most dramatic fellsides in the district and the crags below the summit ridge are nearly a mile long. But my friend is by no means alone in not knowing about this long line of crag, as big as several Napes Ridges crowded together, for rock-climbers had missed it for fifty years and only started making climbs there about a dozen years ago.

Seen from the valley the crags look almost insignificant because of the length and steepness of the fellside below them, and it is only when you get among them that you realize what you have been missing. The crag is not among the best in Lakeland, but at least there's a lot of it, the rock is good, and some of the climbs, particularly on the Great Nose and the Pillar, are quite impressive. So far about twenty routes have been made and there's scope for more new climbing there, although the approaches to the crag—for the climber—can be rather long and tedious.

But there's much more to St. Sunday Crag than this rather restricted appeal for the rock-climber. For the mountain is not only a shapely, impressive fell but a magnificent viewpoint. The summit itself, as I have indicated, is rather dull, but from a point a little way down towards the north, and indeed from almost any point along this north-east ridge, there are wonderful views of Ullswater—perhaps the best views of the lake you can get from any of the surrounding fells. And the descent from the summit down this long ridge, across the shoulder of Birks, and through the steeply wooded slopes of Glemara Park is among the particular joys of a visit to Patterdale. This is a track for walking down rather than up, for the view is below you all the way—the lake curving round the side of Place Fell, with its tiny islands riding like yachts at anchor, and the scene slowly changing from crag and woodland to the quiet pastoral beauty of the eastern end.

The hard way up St. Sunday Crag is to plough up the rather dreary zigzags from Elmhow in Grisedale, and this is the way the climber goes, but there is quite an interesting route from Deepdale by way of the east ridge, or better still, the mountain can be approached from Fairfield. I suppose I must have come off Fairfield this way dozens of times—over Cofa Pike, down to Deepdale Hause and then, pleasantly and easily, over the top of St. Sunday and down to Patterdale for food and drink. Alternatively, the walker can get his peak the long, easy way by walking

up Grisedale to the tarn, and then working his way up the screes
to Deepdale Hause and on to the summit with the run down to
Patterdale as dessert.

Before the rock-climbers found the crag, the Grisedale face of
the mountain used to be an interesting place for wild flowers,
perhaps because hardly anybody ever went there. I hope and
believe it will continue so, for the climbs are not likely to attract
crowds of Great Gable proportions, and you can still have them
to yourself and watch the processions moving over Striding
Edge across the valley. Perhaps we've been on the crags half a
dozen times, but we've never seen anybody else there.

Although the actual summit of St. Sunday Crag is not an
especially interesting place and only a moderate viewpoint the
neighbouring top of Gavel Pike, across a little saddle, is a
pleasant, airy peak well worth a visit. One rewarding view from
the main summit—perhaps its main feature—is the splendid
peep into the coves below the summit of Helvellyn, but the bulk
of this mountain, and of Fairfield, too, prevents many distant
views. The sweeps down into Grisedale and Deepdale, however,
maintain St. Sunday Crag's dominance, and the views to the
north-east, once the descent is begun, will always justify the
climb to the top.

The last time we came down from St. Sunday Crag the long
lake looked like a silver scimitar curving round the shoulder of
Place Fell and the air was so still we could see the Scots pines
reflected in the waters of Lanty Tarn in the little col on the edge
overlooking Glenridding. The dogs were barking down at
Grassthwaite How but the Grisedale Beck was silent and we
could see no movement, except for the clouds, over the whole
countryside. Down in the woods the leaves were turning to gold
and the smoke from the cottages in Patterdale rose straight and
slowly in the evening air.

Red Screes

Red Screes is an easy, descriptive name for the friendly whale-
backed giant that mounts guard over Kirkstone Pass. You can
see the screes from the inn and the colour is particularly striking
when the sun comes out after rain. Here is a forthright, uncomplicated sort of mountain, with four distinct sides—a long gentle
ridge, a steeper ridge, a grassy incline, and a craggy face. The
summit, when you come to think of it, probably lies closer to a
main road than any other major mountain in Lakeland, being

less than half a mile from the top of the pass and little more than a thousand feet higher, but it is a surprisingly neglected fell. Thousands of people, noticing it on the skyline from heights around Kendal, could not give it a name and the mountain is unsung by many of the guide-book writers. Indeed, some of the maps even get it wrong, naming the mountain Kilnshaw Chimney and reserving the name Red Screes for the northern slopes dropping towards Patterdale.

Several years ago the Queen, on her first visit to the Lake District, was driven over Kirkstone Pass and under the crags of Red Screes but we do not know whether the mountain was pointed out to her, or whether, like many thousands of other visitors, before and after her, she just glanced at the bulky fell, promptly forgetting all about it and reserving her interest for the panorama of Windermere opening out below.

This seems to be the trouble with Red Screes—taken overmuch for granted and not nearly so often explored as its nearness to roads might indicate. For, if you were really pressed, you could have your lunch in the Kirkstone Pass Inn, run up and down the mountain, and be back down for a drink in an hour, and I can't think of any other Lake District mountain that could be so easily humbled. The summits of Dale Head and Eskdale's Harter Fell are not far from motor roads but not so close to civilization as Red Screes and nothing like so near to alcoholic refreshment. I must have driven over Kirkstone hundreds of times, but can hardly ever remember seeing people scrambling up the mountain from the roadside and there's no track that I can recall.

Of course, many hundreds of people do the long trudge up the fell from Ambleside and a few go up the rather more rewarding ascent from Patterdale, later descending, perhaps, the uninteresting western slopes into Scandale and ignoring altogether the mountain's eastern face which is its principal glory. Somebody once wrote that Red Screes looked from the south and east like a steeply breaking wave and it is a good description. The mountain has something of this appearance from my house and the impression is heightened under snow with the dark crags showing like shadows under the white wave. With its plateau-like summit ridge Red Screes always looks to me like a good mountain with the top sawn off. Millions of years ago it might have been a very fine mountain indeed.

Red Screes forms the western wall of Kirkstone Pass as you go up 'The Struggle' from Ambleside but the most dramatic view is from the Windermere entrance to the pass, when you suddenly find yourself driving right up to the wall. It looks impregnable, especially in winter-time, but the average walker will scramble up quite easily, threading his way through one or other of the twin combes and between the crags to the summit. Even the late Mr. Baddeley, writing more than half a century ago, admitted that this ascent was "quite practicable and far more exhilarating" than the ordinary route.

But accidents can happen in these rough places and I remember once taking part in the evening rescue of a young man who had fallen in the screes below Raven Crag, which overlooks the southern of the two combes, and injured himself badly. It was a difficult job manhandling the stretcher down the shattered fell-side and trying to get the young fellow down to the waiting doctor in the growing darkness. A boulder that fell from one of these crags on the eastern face of Red Screes hundreds or thousands of years ago gave Kirkstone Pass its name. Many visitors fail to notice this boulder but if they look about fifty yards to the left side of the road just as the pass begins to dip down to Patterdale they will spot it. The top of the boulder bears some resemblance to a ridged church tower and you can easily climb to the top.

Kilnshaw Chimney which some map-makers have confused with the summit is a rather disappointing affair—a narrow, scree-choked gully running down from the summit and bearing no resemblance whatever to a household chimney. I suppose it could be said to have some slight association with the sort of chimney that climbers know—although much wider and not nearly so steep. But curiously enough the mountain *does* carry a very fair imitation of a household chimney stuck on a sloping roof if it is viewed from near the foot of the pass on the Brotherswater side. Many years ago, before I was finally persuaded that Kilnshaw Chimney was the scree-filled gully, I used to think that it might have been this impression of a chimney near the roof of the mountain that led to the name. For, I argued, household chimneys have had much the same shape for many hundreds of years, whereas rock-climbers have only been talking about *their* sort of chimneys for a hundred years or so.

Among the best things about Red Screes are the summit and the view. The highest of the several summit cairns is a big mound of stones dumped at the edge of the plateau and right on top of the crags, and from hereabouts you feel you could hurl a stone at the inn more than a thousand feet below. The views are very fine, with most of Windermere mapped out below you, a glimpse of the Yorkshire hills to the south-east, an extensive peep into Patterdale, and many of the most shapely Lakeland mountains standing up all around you.

But the most interesting feature of the summit is the presence of a small tarn, and several satellite ponds, no more than twenty yards away. Not many Lakeland summits carry tarns but where they are found they add a refreshing reward for the toil up the fellside and provide fascinating foregrounds to the views. I am told that these tarns on Red Screes rely almost entirely on rainfall, but I have always found the largest one full. Mr. Wainwright, the guide-book writer, claims the tarn has "the highest resident population of tadpoles" and I will not disagree with him, although I've never noticed any there. Perhaps I've been there at the wrong time. He also claims for Red Screes the greatest mileage of stone walls of any fell east of the Keswick to Windermere road, which may well be true for the mountain is surrounded by them, as is also the neighbouring fell of Snarker Pike.

Like many Lakeland mountains Red Screes has two sides completely opposite in character—the dramatic eastern side, with its rocky combes and great banks of crumbling red scree, and its featureless western slopes of grass and marsh land. With a more rugged face to the west Red Screes would be one of the principal mountains in southern Lakeland. But as it is the mountain only really impresses from one side, and has to be content to be no more than a hand-maiden to Fairfield. And a much more suburban mountain than Fairfield—so accessible by main road and with crags that look interesting but prove on closer acquaintance to be too shattered and crumbling for sport. A mountain largely given over to shepherds and sheep and also nowadays to the quarry workings further down on the slopes of Snarker Pike.

Red Screes is a slowly crumbling mountain, for each year a few more tons of rock tumble down from the crags to bestrew the eastern slopes. I like to go up there in winter-time when there's nobody about and sometimes the air so still that you can hear voices down at the Kirkstone Inn. But many, many people going over the pass, winter and summer, never bother even to find out the name of the bulky mountain blocking the view to the west. They just take it for granted.

Seat Sandal

Seat Sandal, wrote the late M. J. B. Baddeley towards the end of last century, was a mountain seldom climbed—"except by those who mistake it for Helvellyn in the summer, or are after the harriers or foxhounds in winter." And the Oracle was not far wrong, for although this is a mountain that everybody sees as they drive along the main highway through Lakeland very few people take the trouble to scramble to the summit. It lies cheek by jowl with the busiest road in Lakeland, is one of the easiest summits in the district to attain and one of the quickest fells to descend but it still remains almost a secret mountain.

We all know Seat Sandal as the long swelling shoulder of fell that soars to a flattish summit from the top of Dunmail Raise and faces Steel Fell across the pass—but little more. Seen from Grasmere the fell presents a perfect symmetry to the northern view—a mountain of gentle curves, softly lit by the evening sun. It is the last hill in Westmorland before you drop down into Cumberland and, some days, into almost a different world.

I must have been across its shoulder a score of times, but I think I've only twice stood on its summit, which is graced, I remember, by three cairns, and I've never seen anybody else walking about on top. Thousands of people walk every summer up the old packhorse track from Grasmere to Grisedale Tarn or up the popular Tongue Gill route, but they rarely turn aside to scramble up the easy slopes on their left to the top of the fell. And the hunts rarely go over the summit for, despite Baddeley, the fox-earths are all much lower down, and the shepherds don't go that way either for the sheep-trods contour the lower slopes. There are no walkers' tracks across the top, and no litter, and if you want to find some peace and quiet on a Bank Holiday I'm sure you'll find it there. So that Seat Sandal seems to be accepted as a mere backcloth to the view, a graceful outlier of little character, a fine viewpoint—although not so good as its neighbour, Fairfield—and little more than a smooth curve of grass and bracken with no surprises.

Much of this is true but Seat Sandal *can* be enjoyed if you use your imagination, for here is a mountain of ghosts. It all goes back a very long time. There was, for instance, Dunmail, the last king of independent Cumberland who, some historians say, was killed on the pass, and his golden crown carried over the mountain to be sunk in the waters of Grisedale Tarn. Once a year, they say, the warriors who carried the crown across the fell and then melted into the mist to await his summons, return to the shoulder of Seat Sandal to recover his circlet from the waters. Gently they lift the crown from the depths and bear it down to the heap of stones on the pass under which, some say, the king's body lies buried. Three times the leader strikes the stones with his spear, but each time comes the answer out of the air: "Not yet, not yet; wait a while, my warriors." And so the phantom army disappears into the mist and fades away for another year. But you can still see the cairn "heaped over brave King Dunmail's bones" hard by the county boundary on the summit of the pass and, if you like, dream your dreams.

There was another ghost, too—a fair female ghost, to whom the king plighted his troth accepting her ring and giving in return his bracelet. And they say that on snowy nights the phantom of the king may sometimes be seen pursuing a spectral maiden until both are swallowed up in the mists that hang over the fell. Perhaps there is also another ghost close to the tarn where, a century and a half ago, William Wordsworth bade a last farewell to his brother John, commander of the East India-man, *Earl of Abergavenny*, who was afterwards drowned with all his crew and passengers off Portland. Grieving over his loss the poet wrote some verses and two of these were later carved on a rock face at the instigation of Canon Rawnsley. The inscription became almost illegible but Joe Bowman, the former huntsman of the Ullswater pack, had a plate, erected by private subscription, let into the rock to tell the story. And they still call the stone The Brothers' Rock.

I have also heard of other Seat Sandal 'ghosts'. An Ulverston lady tells me that she once walked over Seat Sandal from Grise-dale Tarn with a friend. Ahead of them, but always just out of sight, they could hear two men talking, and from time to time they heard a dog barking. All the way up the steep grassy slope they could hear the men and their dog just ahead, and keeping their distance, and they fully expected to see them at any moment. But when they reached the summit and could see for miles around and all the way down the other side, there was just no one there. The men—and the dog—had vanished in the mountain air.

But Seat Sandal is not only ghosts and grass and bracken. It runs to rock, too, at its eastern end just as you round the fell on your way to Grisedale Tarn. Here is a mass of tumbled rock and scree topped by an overhanging crag—in sharp contrast to the mild western slopes but a contrast that is common to many

Lakeland mountains. There is, indeed, a climbing hut on Dunmail Raise, but I don't think anybody ever goes climbing here with so many more rewarding places not far away. Another interesting feature about Seat Sandal is that its waters pass into Morecambe Bay by way of Grasmere and Windermere, into the Solway Firth by way of Ullswater and the Eden, into the Irish Sea by Thirlmere and the Derwent, or, into industrial Lancashire down the aqueduct. It is thus claimed that its waters reach the sea at more widely divergent points than those of any other Lakeland fell.

The 1-inch Ordnance Survey map gives two Seat Sandals—the other one on the north side of Raise Beck on the western slopes of Dollywaggon Pike, although I've always known this fellside as Willie Wife Moor. It could be that the map-makers have slipped up here. The county boundary goes up Raise Beck so that the mountain is entirely in Westmorland. Probably the easiest way up Seat Sandal is the lazy trudge from the top of Dunmail Raise, up Raise Beck for some distance, and then straight up the slope to the summit cairn but you can reach the top from almost any direction without much difficulty. The best views from the summit are to the west and many lakes and tarns are clearly seen, not least Thirlmere which looks especially attractive from here.

Nowadays the mountain is included in the Lakeland twenty-four hours record and Eric Beard, of Leeds, who ran up and down fifty-six mountains within the day in 1963, reached the summit from Fairfield in exactly twenty-eight minutes, descending to Dunmail Raise in a further nineteen minutes. And this was at night! Two years later Alan Heaton of Accrington who topped no fewer than sixty mountains within twenty-four hours went from the top of Dollywaggon Pike to Seat Sandal summit in half an hour and was down on Dunmail fifteen minutes later. He found the grass wet and slippery running down and thought he should have done it more quickly. Lesser mortals will take much longer.

Seat Sandal can be a disappointing guide to skiers. Being smooth and grassy it holds the slightest snow-fall easily and seen from afar with the morning sun glistening on the thin covering one can easily be led into thinking that the fells are well plastered. I've been caught this way myself more than once until I learned better.

I can't really pretend that Seat Sandal is a favourite mountain. It has a graceful outline and its ghosts, but little else although, truth to tell, every Lakeland fell is a wonderful place at the right time. And the right time for Seat Sandal, the late W. T. Palmer, who knew it as well as anybody, used to say is at night. Perhaps some time a trip up Seat Sandal by moonlight to see the sunrise, as a change from Helvellyn, might be worthwhile. You never know what you might see up there, if you're in the right frame of mind.

7

QUIET HILLS

(East of Kirkstone)

High Street

THE Ill Bell range, including Froswick and Yoke was once traversed—just below the summits—by a motor-cycle but no modern vehicle, to the best of my knowledge, has ever rattled along Lakeland's High Street. Some of us may be thankful for this and yet, nearly two thousand years ago, the Romans who built this wild highway in the clouds, went along it in their chariots or in slave-borne litters.

We don't think of High Street as a road today but to the Romans it was, I suppose, a main highway across the mountains for their horses and troops from Carlisle to Galava, which the Norsemen renamed Hamel Saetr and we call Ambleside. And it was the Romans, or rather their British and foreign slaves, who hauled thousands of tons of rock, much of it sandstone, right up to the ridge and then hacked out and laid the road which you can still trace today. It runs something like fifteen miles along the eastern roof of what is now the National Park—most of it at more than two thousand feet above sea-level.

High Street is the name of the old Roman highway across the fells and also of the highest mountain along the range. Fewer than a score of Lakeland mountains are higher than this impressive plateau and none of them have a longer story. For centuries after the Romans had gone, marauding brigands and raiding Scots crept along the summit ridge and later still the dalesfolk held horse-races up there accompanied, it is said, by drinking carousels which went on for days. You need a little imagination to get the best out of the top of High Street. If you have none, it is just a dull plateau with a survey column stuck on top and pleasant views all round. But it is worthwhile to sit down for a while on a sunny afternoon when perhaps the larks are singing, and try and picture the ancient Britons who knew these slopes and built their homes and their forts in the surrounding valley heads. And then the Romans, marching along the ridge between their garrisons at Brougham and Ambleside, the Scots invaders fighting their way to the top and, in more recent times, the dalesmen at their annual sports. They must have had tremendous energy, these ancestors of ours. Men from Mardale and Longsleddale and even further afield used to drag barrels of beer and mountains of food up the fellside, and then race their horses along the grassy ridges, or get down to the wrestling.

You can still see where the road went, nearly all the way from Troutbeck Park, east of Ambleside, to Celleron, south of Penrith. The faint track which goes up the steep side of Froswick from Troutbeck Park, once a deer preserve and now a Herdwick sheep farm, is known as the 'Scots' Rake' for this is the way the raiders from the north came down from the heights. Once on the ridge you carry on north-east for the summit of High Street, and it is believed that two great stones, still lying on the ground, might have marked the way. The actual summit ridge of High Street is skirted to the west by the Roman road which then swings eastwards towards High Raise, steering between the crags of Rampsgill Head and Kidsty Pike. This is fine, wild country with steep drops into the surrounding valleys, but armies must have come this way, rounding the crags high up above deep tarns, and pressing on remorselessly nor'-nor'-east for Penrith and the Border. And after this the way continues, with not so much excitement, over Wether Hill and Loadpot and Moor Divock and on, if you like, to Pooley Bridge and a new county.

Among the more rewarding features of High Street are the valleys scooped into its flanks—Riggindale, Randale Beck, Rampsgill, Measand Beck, Fusedale, Cawdale, Heltondale, Hayeswater and the rest. These are the places, and not so much the ridge itself, which give the area its character, but not many people go into these dales and their high corries now that Haweswater is a reservoir and Mardale almost a dead valley. And on the other side of the range there is the deer sanctuary with restricted access, so that these quiet, unspoiled valleys are among the least-visited places in the National Park.

But these deep troughs under High Street, being so untracked, are the home of much of the wild life, both flora and fauna, of Lakeland. One recent writer describes how he looked out of his hotel bedroom in Mardale towards High Street and counted, across the mirrored waters of the lake early one morning, twelve Fell ponies, twenty-six sheep and six red deer. And this is by no means surprising. I think it was on High Street that I saw my first red deer—the first to be clearly recognized as such—and I certainly saw my first Fell ponies up there. The deer—three or four of them—had just climbed out of Riggindale and were silhouetted for a moment on the ridge between High Street and The Knott. They would have made a superb colour-picture, sharply outlined against the westering sun, but people didn't take colour pictures in those days. For a few seconds they stood there, poised and relaxed after their climb and unaware that we were standing a few yards away. And then they must have caught our scent and, in a flash, were bounding away down the steep slopes towards Hayeswater.

On another early visit I came upon the Fell ponies grazing just below The Knott—wild, shaggy creatures looking much too fierce to be stroked. There were about a dozen of them and we youngsters walked among them, as near as we dared, admiring their rough coats and long tails. In those days these might well have been wild Fell ponies but nowadays, although many still roam the same fells untended all are in some sort of private ownership, perhaps of the Lord of the Manor. Buzzards and ravens also haunt these upland crags and the higher coves contain some of the rarer plants of Lakeland. It was in this area, near Gray Crag, one of the outliers of High Street, where I once saw what I believe was the rare rough-legged buzzard. I kept him in view for some time and later saw him fly into a tree near Pasture Beck where, perhaps, he intended to spend the night.

When I first went up High Street as a youngster I used to think it was outside the Lake District. Most of the fells to the east of Kirkstone seemed in those days remote from the best of Lakeland and this impression used to be heightened by the view from the top of the High Street plateau of most of our favourite mountains stretched out along the horizon from the north-west to the south-west. While to a rock-climber the smooth grassy fells seemed to lack the character of more precipitous places. But as the years went by I found new wonders in these neglected hills and made the discovery that High Street is really a mountain of charm and individuality with its fascinating history and surprises round many a corner.

There are many ways up High Street but undoubtedly the best is from Haweswater. You simply leave your car at the end of the reservoir and climb along the ridge of Rough Crag to the tiny tarn at Gospel Gate and then straight up the pleasant rocks of Long Stile to the summit—a wonderful airy walk with fine views all the time leftwards to Blea Water and right to Riggindale, where you may spot red deer. Everything below you is in sight including, of course, the length of Haweswater with Blea Water—probably the deepest tarn in Lakeland—on the other side of the ridge. Only two lakes—Wastwater and Windermere —are deeper, and it has been plumbed to more than two hundred feet. Blea Water is a fine mountain tarn, and just over the little ridge of Piot Crag is Small Water, one of the loveliest pools in the district, with the old packhorse track of the Nan Bield Pass circling its very edge.

As I write I can see the top of the Nan Bield through my study window and can easily picture from memory how it zigzags down the other side and round the tarn. Nearly forty years ago, as I have written, I used to think these eastern hills were not really very exciting, but how wrong I was. Further left, in the view from my window, is the beginning of the ridge where the Romans went. It looks quiet and peaceful up there now but it has not always been so. High Street has had its adventures down the years. Never write it off as a dull mountain.

Harter Fell (Mardale)

Mardale's Harter Fell is a lonely, grassy dome which, from most angles, seems to have little distinction except height. I can see it from my house—an apparently featureless, upland waste just to the right of the gap of Nan Bield—and from Longsleddale or from the Shap Fells road it looks equally uninteresting. But drive into Mardale and look at its northern face and Harter Fell suddenly leaps into focus and becomes a grand mountain. Almost all the worthwhile features of the mountain are concentrated into this rocky northern face which lies between the twin passes of Nan Bield and Gatescarth. Here are great crags split by gullies, a tumbled wilderness of scree, dancing becks with waterfalls splashing over rocky steps, and the lovely gem of Small Water, one of the most perfect tarns in Lakeland.

This is the view of Harter Fell that matters—the view from

the upper reaches of Haweswater or perhaps from one of the High Street ridges. None of the other views do justice to a bold mountain that sees few visitors since Manchester took over the Mardale watershed. Many years ago we used to climb Harter Fell Gully, the black cleft that bites into the main crag from near the sheepfold half-way up the Gatescarth Beck, as a wet day's expedition, but I can't ever remember meeting anybody on the mountain. Sometimes we have gone up the mountain in winter-time to ski down the long drifts above Wren Gill, but we've always had the mountain to ourselves. Once we met a party of farmers on a fox-shoot working their way like beaters across the grassy southern slopes, but they were local men, not visitors. The average Lakeland tourist doesn't know Westmorland's Harter Fell and has perhaps only heard of the Cumberland one to which it bears no resemblance whatever. So that Mardale Harter Fell is essentially a lonely mountain and largely untracked, with route-finding problems in bad weather.

I seem to remember sometimes being able to pick out the little woods around Kendal from the summit, and it is certainly true that the mountain is the culmination of many miles of gently rising ground that mount in easy steps all the way from the River Kent. It would make a fine upland walk from Potter Fell to Harter, with the trough of Longsleddale down on the right for comfort along the way, and perhaps a return down Kentmere. But few people bother with this sort of thing nowadays when you can get nearly as high in half an hour by tripping up, say, Dale Head from the top of Honister.

Small Water lies in a tiny basin, caught between the crags and the pass of Nan Bield, where once the pack-horses went over from Kentmere to Mardale. There is a little shingle beach and a boulder of white quartz beside it, and great rocks tumbled down from the crags lie littered around. A small stream drops down to the tarn from Black John Hole nearly half a mile to the south and Small Water Beck falls away to the east underneath the big crags, cascading down through the rowans and the ash to the lake. Quite close to the tarn are some tiny stone shelters and the tarn contains trout with curious bright red markings. Late July, they say, is the best time to fish for them. Perhaps the tarn is seen at its best in storm when the dark pool among black crags can look an awe-inspiring place but on a sunny morning, with the birds singing and the surface flecked with gold, Small Water is a lovely, peaceful place as those who have camped by its shores will confirm.

Red Screes and Kirkstone Pass

High Street range from Gatescarth Pass
(Harter Fell in shadow on left) (overleaf)

The crags of Harter Fell do not lend themselves to climbing, the gully being the only recorded route in the area. The rock is loose and crumbling and at Wren Gill, on the other side of the mountain, the old quarries are shattered and unattractive. You used to be able to bed down for the night in some comfort in the old abandoned cottages at the quarries if you were exploring in these parts, but I'm told that the roofs have now fallen in so that the accommodation may not be quite so desirable.

If you are ascending the mountain from Longsleddale there is a particularly fine view of the length of Haweswater just after you have crossed over the shoulder of Adam Seat, and, when descending by this route, an almost equally excellent view of Longsleddale from just below the boundary stone. Other routes to the top are from Kentmere by way of Nan Bield or over Kentmere Pike, and from Mardale, this last being a fine short expedition, with close-up views of the crags.

The top of Harter Fell is flat and grassy and the cairn itself disfigured by a jumble of iron fence posts and railings stuck among the stones. But this and the ugly white line which sometimes shows around the shores of Haweswater, Manchester's second Lakeland reservoir, are the only alien sights from the lonely summit ridge. The views extend from Blencathra to the Kent estuary and Morecambe Bay, and from Ingleborough and the Pennines to the Scafells.

I'm afraid that Manchester must be blamed for much of Harter Fell's neglect. For few people go into the hills from Mardale nowadays and the flock-masters no longer travel the passes as they used to do. So that the mountain remains a pleasant sanctuary for a few Kendal and Kentmere folk, an unspoiled area in winter for snatching an hour or two on skis or a quiet place to make for on a sunny Sunday when the processions are inching their way up Great Gable or Helvellyn. But how long these eastern fells will continue to remain 'undiscovered' when the motorway pushes through Westmorland and the highways through the National Park become even too crowded for the gregarious, remains to be seen.

The Troutbeck Fells

The switchback skyline you see on your right as you climb Kirkstone Pass from Windermere provides perhaps the best ridge walk in eastern Lakeland and one of the neatest progressions of little hills in the country. These shapely fells begin

8

Harter Fell and Haweswater
The Helvellyn range from High Street (facing)

beyond the Garburn Pass which winds over the commons between Troutbeck and Kentmere, and then continue north towards High Street. We call them Yoke, Ill Bell, Froswick and Thornthwaite Crag and they have no collective name so far as I know, although I have always known them as the Troutbeck Fells. Strangely—for their more dramatic slopes drop steeply into Kentmere—they seem to belong to Troutbeck, perhaps because we see them so often as we motor northwards over Kirkstone. So that, unlike many other examples in Lakeland, it is really the *back* of these fells that is the rugged side.

The Romans knew these hills well for they went with their pack-horses up the hillside from the little side-valley behind Troutbeck Park to the northern end of the ridge and then north-east over High Street. You can still trace their route up Hagg Gill and then by way of what we now know as the Scots' Rake to the ridge near Thornthwaite Crag. They wore the grooves you can still see up the steep flank of Froswick with their traffic, and their way across the plateau to High Street, which must have been difficult in mist, was marked by two great stones still lying on the ground. Then across the broad backbone of High Street went the Romans, perhaps with carts or chariots or litters carried by slaves, past the steep drop to Blea Water and Riggindale on their right and Hayeswater far below to the left, and on to the sharp peak of Kidsty Pike. And thereafter the way is plain to see and easy to follow, as they carried on to High Raise, Red Crag and Wether Hill and eventually to Moor Divock and its sepulchral cairns, and so to the toe of Ullswater and the Eden plain.

But whether the Romans would notice from their high road the splendid view to the south that is the special glory of these fells I could not guess. Perhaps they weren't interested in scenery but only in getting across a wild, foreign land as quickly as possible. The modern traveller, though, should preferably walk the ridge from the north after perhaps winning his height by way of the Scots' Rake which is also the way the raiders from the north might have come along after the Romans had left. For from both Thornthwaite Crag and Ill Bell some of the finest panoramic views of southern Lakeland, including the long length of Windermere, may be enjoyed. When the sunshine is flooding the southern half of the National Park you look down on a sparkling picture of silvery waters, neat woodlands and bright meadows. You cannot see the crowds and the traffic and not much of the towns and villages so that it all looks unspoiled and prettily pastoral. And as you walk the ridge this pleasant prospect is always ahead of you while over to your right are the Coniston Fells and, further away, Black Combe and the estuary of the Duddon.

I can see the Troutbeck hills, end-on, from my house—first, the great bulk of Yoke with the black precipice of Rainsborrow Crag dropping down into Kentmere, and then the shapely cone of Ill Bell behind and, a little to the east, the summit of Thornthwaite Crag with its 14-feet high beacon clearly visible on the best days. Froswick is out of sight behind Ill Bell, but if I can see the beacon clearly on a summer's evening there is a fair chance it will rain next day.

The best-known view of these fells, however, is from the Kirkstone road where you can see them all from top to toe— smooth grassy slopes dropping steeply to the Trout Beck with the ridge itself, especially under snow, looking rather like a blown sail leaning backwards against the sky. You can go straight up the fells from this side but it's hard work; far better to come down this way, exploring the old quarry workings as you do so. But if the familiar view lacks drama, that from the opposite side—the Kentmere side—is wild enough for here the steep slopes break into crags that look dark and savage against the westering sun. This is the usual feature of a Lakeland ridge —smooth slopes on one side and on the other, the northern or eastern side, the fellside carved into combes and hanging valleys with crags and buttresses in between.

Ill Bell, perhaps the best known of these fells, is one of the most graceful and beautifully shaped hills in Lakeland. From certain angles it really *is* shaped like a bell, symmetric and rounded, and this is almost certainly the derivation of the name. But Ill has nothing to do with 'hill' although the mountain is named Hill Bell on the two-and-a-half-inch Ordnance Survey map and was so named in the guide-books of a hundred years ago. The most likely derivative is Eel or E'il, meaning evil. You can find the same word in several parts of Lakeland—Eel Tarn, Eel Crags, Ill Crag and so on, supposedly dark and foreboding places, although I've never found them so. And the word has nothing to do with eels, either.

One of the most interesting features of Ill Bell is its multiplicity of cairns. I've never counted them, but there must be half a dozen quite large piles and several smaller ones as well. They are scattered right across the summit so that, in mist, you are always stumbling into them without knowing exactly where you are, but their presence, although sometimes a nuisance, gives the mountain quite a distinctive appearance when seen from afar. From Dove Crag, Fairfield or Red Screes, for instance, the cairns look like the crumbled remains of towers and when you spot them from these or other tops you know immediately you are looking at Ill Bell, for no other Lakeland mountain has this characteristic. Why they were built in such profusion on a modest summit less than 2,500 feet high I cannot guess, but they are quite fine specimens of their kind and greatly superior to the ugly heaps that litter the approaches to Gable and Scafell.

Less than two miles away to the north-east is another Ill Bell —Mardale Ill Bell, set on a spur of High Street that looks down on the lovely tarns of Blea Water and Small Water. Strange there should be two hills of the same name so close to each other, for they have little in common. Mardale Ill Bell is not much more than an outlier of High Street, except on its north-eastern side where it has several dramatic features. Here you may see red deer and Fell ponies but you are unlikely to do so on the Troutbeck Fells.

Froswick is a remarkable replica of Ill Bell, although cast in a rather smaller mould, while Yoke is rather a dull, sprawling mountain except on its Kentmere side where it is a mass of crag that has never produced any rock-climbing worthy of the name as it is so loose. But Rainsborrow Crag is a rare place for foxes. Most people go to Ill Bell by way of Yoke but, as I have said, it is better to go up by the Scots' Rake and then come back over Yoke with the views in front. Thornthwaite Crag, overlooking four fine valleys, is a splendid viewpoint, and as the summit is readily seen from many directions, has long been a beacon. The column on the summit is one of the best-built cairns in Lakeland and may be climbed by the agile.

I find the Troutbeck Fells easy, accommodating hills, so easy, in fact, that, as I have written earlier, a motor-cyclist once traversed much of their length, although not over the tops. To walk along them in autumn when the colours are changing or in winter, with snow on the ground and the distant views sharp and inviting, is one of the best things to do with a free day from Windermere or Ambleside. You can start in the valley that was once a deer park, do the round in an afternoon and, from the ridge, see most of the best of eastern Lakeland.

Caudale Moor

As you drive over the top of Kirkstone Pass and dip down towards Patterdale you will see the skirts of a considerable mountain sweeping down on your right but, unless you are one of a small minority, you will feel no particular urge to seek out its summit. Indeed, most people neither know the name of the mountain nor care much about it for—like Helvellyn from the Thirlmere road—there's little challenge in its shape and you'll hardly ever see people going up there. To most people it is probably just a great lump of fellside, not to be compared with, for instance, the craggy front of Red Screes that faces it across the pass. And, ten to one, you won't find the mountain mentioned in the guide-books while some of the maps don't even seem to be certain about its name.

But Caudale Moor—for that is its name—is really quite a fine mountain despite its disappointing appearance from the main road, and its 2,500-feet-high summit may be reached more easily than most others in Lakeland. For you've only a thousand feet or so to make from the inn at the top of the pass and, although this is not an especially attractive ascent, you should be able to get to the cairn in about three-quarters of an hour. And yet very few people seem to bother to go up there, so that if you want to find solitude on a day when the pass is choc-a-bloc with cars, and Gable and Helvellyn swarming with people, Caudale Moor could be one of the places to make for. But preferably I suggest you should go there in winter when you can really savour the desolation and loneliness of unspoiled fells where the red deer and the Fell ponies and the foxes roam undisturbed. It was on Caudale Moor, just above Threshthwaite Mouth, where, for half an hour, I once watched a fox taking his ease in the snow and quietly walking about his own back garden. Even when he spotted me he didn't run away but merely ambled slowly up the screes, his long brush sweeping the snow as he carefully zigzagged the fellside.

Some people know the mountain as John Bell's Banner but this name, I suggest, really only applies to the lower summit of the moor. The actual summit is Stony Cove Pike—a little cairn on a rather desolate plateau, with grey rock here and there outcropping the grass. Many people have wondered who on earth John Bell could have been, and I think I can tell them. Almost certainly he was the Rev. John Bell, curate and school-master of Ambleside, who lived from 1553 to 1620. Banner is the old word for boundary and since at one time the parishes of Windermere, Grasmere and Patterdale met on the top of Caudale Moor it is probable that the summit or thereabouts became known locally as the limit of the sphere of Mr. Bell's ministrations, this being before the days when Ambleside became a separate parish. There would, of course, be other John Bells—a fairly common name—and another suggestion is that the name could have a hunting derivation—the place where John Bell had to try to turn the quarry during a hunt. But I think this an unlikely explanation. Anyway, the name is still preserved on the maps of the Ordnance Survey.

Quite close to the lower summit is a cairn topped by a cross. This is the Mark Atkinson monument and it was erected by his son, Mr. Ion Atkinson, who still lives at Sykeside, Brothers-water, in memory of his father who died nearly forty years ago. Mark Atkinson was a well-known farmer and also the licensee of the Kirkstone Pass Inn, which his son still owns. Before he died he expressed a wish that his ashes should be laid to rest near the summit of Caudale Moor at a place looking out over the pass and the valley he knew so well. Mr. Atkinson owned that part of the fell and his son later added to the holding but recently it was acquired by the National Trust, so that Caudale Moor now belongs to the nation.

For all its tame appearance from the Kirkstone road the mountain is really a complicated mass of considerable character, with several craggy ridges running off in different directions. Its subsidiary summits include Hartsop Dodd, Hart Crag, Pike How and St. Raven's Edge, while Caudale Head is a fine rocky cirque and Raven Crag, overlooking the lovely valley of Pasture Beck, one of the steepest crags in the district. Many years ago, when I was much more agile than I am today, two of us spent many weekends trying to force climbing routes up the over-hangs on this crag, but we never completed anything worth-while. There is the possibility of a sensational traverse right across the cliff and parallel to the screes but it means resorting to artificial aids and in those days we thought twice about knocking pitons into Lakeland rock. Perhaps the young experts of today could do something with it.

If you include all its outliers Caudale Moor is really one of the most extensive mountains in Lakeland, embracing all the area between Kirkstone Pass, Pasture Beck and the Trout Beck. From the valley you might think Hartsop Dodd a fine conical peak, but when you come to climb it you discover it is merely part of one of the ridges of Caudale Moor and hardly a mountain in its own right.

Seen from the head of the Troutbeck valley Caudale Moor comes into its own as a splendid rocky mountain and you may wonder, seeing it from this angle for the first time, why you've never bothered to explore it. The walk round the mountain is at least ten miles but a pleasant half-day may be enjoyed by going for the summit by way of the steep ridge that drops down to Brotherswater, descending by the east side of the fell to Threshthwaite Mouth and thence down either Pasture Beck or the Trout Beck and back to the main road over the pass. Threshthwaite Mouth is a fascinating gap in the hills and can be quite an exciting place in bad weather or snow. Caudale Moor is an interesting mountain to negotiate on skis but the descent to this gap sometimes proves awkward.

There are ancient settlements down on the Trout Beck side of the moor, a deserted quarry on the north side, some old mine workings above Hartsop, and a cluster of tiny tarns near the summit but few tracks lie across the moor which is criss-crossed by a maze of stone walls. I once found a Government bench-mark on one of these walls, left there, no doubt, by surveyors, but there's no other sign of man except for the old sheepfolds, for the mountain has been grazed for centuries and the farmers still keep some of the walls in reasonable repair.

The views from the top—or better still, from the shoulders, since the summit is too flat—are very beautiful, especially in winter-time when the crags are shown up to best advantage. There are not many trees on these fells nowadays but they say that, long years ago, a squirrel could have passed from the edge of Windermere to the rocks at Threshthwaite Mouth without touching the ground. The last time I was on the mountain I had gone up on skis from the Kirkstone Inn and saw red deer down in Woundale and, at the end of the day, an old buzzard sitting in a tree near Brotherswater.

To me, Caudale Moor has always been a winter mountain and there's no more satisfying end to a cold, bracing day on these bleak mountain sides than to come down the perfect little valley of Pasture Beck at dusk, sniff the woodsmoke from the first farms, see the lights come on at the houses in Low Hartsop, and make one's way towards food, drink and warmth. Secretly, of course, I'm glad that Caudale Moor is a neglected mountain, for it's not really a place for crowds.

Place Fell

It was a wild, windy day with the clouds well down on the higher mountains when I was last on Place Fell. I had just reached the little rocky protuberance of The Knight and was making for the summit when I happened to look round and saw about ten red deer trot sedately along the track that leads up from Boardale, across the top of the fell and down towards the shattered rocks of Grey Crag overlooking the lake. There must be bad weather on the way, I thought, for they say in Patterdale that when the red deer from Martindale appear over the skyline of Place Fell they can expect the worst. And, sure enough, before I had got back to Kendal the sky was choked with angry black clouds, the trees tossing madly in the gale, the birds almost blown out of the sky and the rain dashing relentlessly against the car windows. It remained stormy for days and I wondered whether the deer had found sanctuary in time.

You can often find red deer on Place Fell, for it is only two or three miles away from their home in Martindale, which has been a deer forest for hundreds of years. Sometimes the people of Patterdale, snuggled under the side of the fell, can hear them roaring, and now and again the deer will swim the lake and go adventuring into Cumberland.

But there are many other exciting things besides deer about Place Fell—a proud, bulky mountain worthy of much more attention than its modest height would suggest. For example, the fell is the ideal grandstand from which to spy out the eastern half of Lakeland. Set neatly within the southern curve of Ullswater, Place Fell dominates the head of the lake and the villages of Patterdale and Glenridding much more than the higher mountains of the Helvellyn range. It has an air of detachment, superiority almost, as if to suggest that although not very high it can still hold its own with most other fells in the area. And so it can. Its broad-shouldered massiveness, the steepness of its sides plunging straight into the lake or down towards lonely Boardale, and its lack of direct connection with the surrounding loftier peaks, give it a dignity not often found in such a relatively low hill. For Place Fell, despite its bulky outline and rugged slopes, is not half the height of Ben Nevis.

I don't know whether many people go up Place Fell. Certainly the valleys to the east—the red deer country—are among the least visited in Lakeland, and the Ordnance Survey 1-inch map shows only one main track across its slopes. You will never find crowds up there and as often as not the mountain will be deserted. During my last three visits spread over a couple of years I don't think I've seen more than half a dozen people. And the last time there were only the red deer and a pair of ravens, noisily circling the summit.

Yet, despite this neglect of the mountain itself—a circumstance which does not displease me—there is, on its lower slopes, a walk that has more than once been described as the most beautiful in Lakeland. Indeed, one old guide, published more than half a century ago, described it as the finest walk in the country and I only hope that my praise will not result in its being spoiled by the thoughtless. For this lake-shore walk from Sandwick (where the road on the Westmorland side of the lake comes to an end) to Patterdale is four miles of perfection and variety and still free from litter and rowdyism, even in summer time. On the right sort of day—either early spring or late autumn are my favourites—the walk is as rewarding as anything in Scotland and comparable with certain lovely lake shore walks I have enjoyed in Austria and Switzerland. Even with mist blanketing the mountain tops, squalls of driving rain and never a gleam of sunshine—the conditions on my last winter visit—it is delightful.

Ideally, you should start at the Sandwick end, for then you get the views, straight ahead, of the valleys gradually opening out across the lake, and the mountains slowly grouping themselves into the perfection of symmetry they achieve when viewed from opposite Glenridding. The path hugs the shore, rising and falling through the birches and here and there skirting the edge of crags that drop sheer into the water. Every few minutes you turn a corner or top a rise to see a new view, a new reach of the lake perhaps, or another valley unfolding its green floor across blue dancing waters.

The more familiar peeps into Grisedale, Glencoynedale and the glen leading up to the old Greenside mines are pleasant when seen from the road, but seen from the opposite side of the lake, nearly a mile away, the pictures seem to leap into perfect focus and take on a new splendour. These are ground-level views for the most part, not views from the heights, but you can't see them from a car, and you don't see them on the picture-postcards. The walk is sufficiently long—eight miles there and back —to deter those not really interested, but a couple of miles stroll out from Patterdale will give the elderly or slightly infirm a good idea of the potential of the trip. But, as often as not, and especially in winter time, you will have the walk to yourself.

This side of Place Fell is remarkably steep and rough and the slopes are most attractively scattered with juniper—splashes of dark green against the heather and the bracken. At the foot of the track and on both sides of it are the birches and the sight of the blue waters of the lake through the straight white trunks is particularly rewarding. Here and there below the track will be seen quiet shingly beaches, and at Silver Point there is an attractive bay and a superb viewpoint from which to view the Patterdale valleys with their surrounding fells. Half-way across the lake is the tiny island of Householme, almost opposite to the entrance to Glencoynedale.

High above the tracks are the rocks of Grey Crag and below the cliff a tumbled mass of broken crags and boulders that could make a fine practice ground for the scrambler. No climbing routes, to the best of my knowledge, have yet been made on Grey Crag, although several interesting possibilities may be spotted from the track, a thousand feet below. From several points near the track it is possible to dive into the lake and the bathing along this unfrequented side of Ullswater can be superb but only good swimmers should go into the water here. The bottom slopes very steeply to a depth of two hundred feet or more and there would be no possibility of speedy rescue if a bather got into difficulties. I well remember once picnicking along this track with my family many years ago. My daughter, then very young, was swimming near the edge when she suddenly discovered she was out of her depth, became alarmed and went under with a gurgle. The ensuing rescue was easy enough but it necessitated my diving in wearing my underpants and in the confusion I neglected to take my pipe out of my mouth. So I had to go in a second time to fish it out.

By all means, therefore, picnic along this delightful shore but be careful in the water, especially the children. There must be dozens of places along this idyllic four miles where you can lie down on perfect turf, look out over most of the length of Ullswater without turning your head and be fairly sure of remaining undisturbed for most of a summer afternoon.

But I realize now that I have written very little about the mountain itself. It is, I think, a mountain to be explored for many of the interesting things are hidden away. You can, for instance, follow the old tracks that cross the fell among the crags or visit the waterfalls in Scalehow Beck or work your way round or over the fell into Boardale. The trudge to the top of the fell from either end is straightforward and easy enough, and the reward more than justifies the effort. From the cairn you can look down on all three reaches of Ullswater and, on a clear day, see the Northern Pennines and perhaps the Lowlands of Scotland. And all the eastern and northern fells of Lakeland, from Helvellyn to High Street and from Skiddaw to Red Screes.

If there is sunshine about you will notice the splendid sculpturing of the valleys across the lake, from Dovedale to Aira Green. Place Fell is the only height I can recall from which you can get this view of parallel valleys mounting upwards to high mountains, each one scooped into saucer-like hollows below circling ridges. And you see this superb picture across the curving reaches of Ullswater, with the houses, farms and hotels of Patterdale and Glenridding looking like toys 2,000 feet below. You can watch the motor cars going through the villages, and this is not a very common feature of a Lakeland mountain view, either.

The best side of Place Fell is the popular front that all the tourists see, but rarely explore. When you have sampled the shore path don't desert this side of the mountain but scramble up the steep sides and find out everything you can, while enjoying the fine views of Ullswater down below your feet. The mountain has three or four tarns just below the summit—all unnamed so far as I know and unmentioned in most guides—while there are beacons on some of the lesser peaks of the ridge, and the prominent rocky feature of The Knight. The descents into Boardale are steep but interesting in places. Foxes have their bields in the crags.

On my last visit to Place Fell I came down from Boardale Hause, past yew trees and pines around the lawns of sturdy, well-built houses nestling into the fellside and then across a trout stream to the evening wood smoke of Patterdale. It was raining, windy and cloudy, but it seemed quiet and peaceful enough around Goldrill Beck, with Place Fell standing guard over the valley. How fortunate, I thought, these people who live under Place Fell beside the river and between the lake and the mountains. They must have the best of all worlds.

8

ALONG THE BACKBONE

(The Helvellyn Range)

Helvellyn

ON A fine summer's day at the height of the 'season' more than six hundred people sometimes find their way to the top of Helvellyn—the most popular mountain summit in the Lake District, and perhaps in England. The figure is given me by the leader of a Brathay Exploration Group party who camped on the top during a wet and windy week in July 1966 and counted everybody who reached the summit. A widespread search for a doctor missing on the Scafells might have kept some walkers away from Helvellyn during the weekend, and another reason for the mountain being comparatively neglected on the Saturday could have been the counter attraction of the World Cup which kept tens of thousands of people glued to their television sets. But on the Tuesday no fewer than 614 people of all shapes and sizes climbed the mountain. The fact that this total was achieved on a weekday in far from perfect weather suggests to me that some weekends when conditions are ideal, perhaps a thousand people have sometimes visited the mountain on a single day. And I'm fairly sure that no other mountain in England can claim anything like this popularity.

Helvellyn, therefore, is the tourists' mountain, *par excellence*. It is also the highest mountain in Lakeland outside the Scafells, the only summit upon which an aeroplane has landed—and taken off again—and the only one of our major fells threatened with a chair-lift to the top. You could say that Helvellyn has been famous for two hundred years or more, although Robert

Morden missed it out altogether from his Lake District map of 1680, preferring to include instead 'Skiddow Hill', 'Hard Knott Hill' and 'Dent Hill' (near Egremont). But for many years, before surveying became a science, Helvellyn was held to be the highest summit in Lakeland and an old doggerel, ignoring the Scafells, went:

"Skiddaw, Lauvellin, and Castican,
Are the highest hills climbed by Englishmen."

For hundreds of people, I suspect, Helvellyn is their *only* mountain—their first and last summit. Old men in Preston and Portsmouth will tell you with pride that they went up Helvellyn in 1895, and hundreds still remember setting off from, say, Grasmere for the ascent and reaching the foot of the mountain by four-in-hand. Many people used to go up on ponies and I have seen a photograph of half a dozen bicycles on the summit. Motor cycles have been up there, too, and the aeroplane made its historic landing near the shelter in 1926.

On the summit, particularly on a fine day, you are quite likely to meet people in ordinary town dress or grandfathers or toddlers or young people in fancy hats. I wouldn't be the least surprised to see a man up there with an umbrella one day or somebody selling lemonade or picture-postards. On one raw December day I met a man of eighty-two on the top. He was carrying, in a waistcoat pocket over his heart, a sort of miniature spirit lamp and explained to me that if it went out he would be dead within the hour, I was very relieved indeed to see the lights of Grasmere as we trotted down together.

But Helvellyn will always for me be "the sunrise mountain". Any fine night or early morning in June—but particularly at weekends—there are likely to be people swarming up this great lump of a fell in the darkness, just for the thrill of watching the dawn come up over the Pennines. Although there are many more impressive mountains in Lakeland than Helvellyn—an uninspiring hump when seen from the main Kendal to Keswick road—it is easy to understand why the top is so popular with the sunrise worshippers. Despite its height it is quickly accessible from the road, easily ascended even in the darkness and commands, from its summit, one of the most extensive views in Lakeland. The summit—an unexciting plateau—may have few of the characteristics of a 'real' mountain top, but from it you may see nearly every mountain in Lakeland and much else besides. The Pennines, for instance, Morecambe Bay, the

Solway Firth, several lakes and tarns and, if you are fortunate, the lowland hills of Scotland.

If you have picked the right sort of morning you will see the eastern sky glowing a rich orange and then gradually the colour will change into flaming red. The first golden rim of the sun then shyly peeps over the Northern Pennines, swells into a great ball of fire, and in a few moments it is a new day and the whole of Lakeland is suddenly flooded with warmth and colour. It is a rewarding sight, well worth the effort, and just the thing to give you an appetite for breakfast. The last time I tried it out—up Striding Edge in the moonlight—I was back home before seven in the morning.

Helvellyn is hardly a mountaineer's mountain, although people have been killed up there. Unlike most of the bigger fells it has no rock climbing on it whatsoever, although I have sometimes thought that a short route might be made on the crag high up on the eastern slopes between Striding and Swirrel Edges. But it would be a long way to go for just one probably indifferent climb. Even in winter the mountain has little in the way of ice-filled gullies to attract the climber, although its cornices can be impressive and its ridges interesting in severe weather. It can be quite a good mountain for the skier, although not nearly so good as the neighbouring summits of White Side and Raise.

But mostly, Helvellyn is the ideal mountain for the modest walker or the novice. There are at least a dozen routes to the top and you are not likely to get lost or injured on any of them, although the ridges may demand some care. The mountain has several interesting, or even remarkable, features. For instance, although it lies half-way along the highest and longest mountain range in Lakeland and is fairly littered with monuments of one sort or another, it has no real summit cairn, but only a small, untidy heap of stones. Elsewhere along the broad, easy paths across the summit plateau there are several quite unnecessary cairns. There is the memorial to the dog that lay for weeks beside its dead master and inspired both Scott and Wordsworth to oft-quoted verse, a memorial on Striding Edge to a fox-hunter, and a stone tablet to commemorate the landing of the aeroplane. When the aircraft took off again it flew, after a run of only a few yards, straight over the crags on the eastern side, just above my suggested rock climb—a feat which must have taken considerable courage, whatever you might think about it as a stunt. Then there is the hidden spring below the summit on the west side of the mountain, the wall shelter (invariably littered with rubbish) where perhaps one awaits the dawn, the disused lead-mines on the western slopes, the sombre depths of Red Tarn, the ruins of the Keppel Cove dam and many other rather unusual mountain features.

But the most remarkable thing about Helvellyn is the complete contrast between its eastern and western sides. To the west the mountain presents an unusually uninteresting side which completely fails to excite the casual traveller coming over Dunmail Raise. Told that the rather dreary fellside above him is the famous Helvellyn the average person, seeing it for the first time, will either decide it's hardly worth a second glance or else think of running to the top for the fun of it the next time he has half an hour to spare. It looks a very easy mountain, particularly from the top of Dunmail, and there's no pointed summit to be seen, and no crags worthy of the name, while the ridge is largely hidden. Just a lot of Christmas trees and, higher up, some grassy slopes with a waterfall or two. Indeed, it surprises me why people who have only seen this side of Helvellyn ever bother to go up.

To the east, however, the Ullswater side, Helvellyn proudly emerges as a mountain of character. Here it is buttressed by fine, lofty ridges and between the ridges are wild, hanging valleys, spattered with crags and waterfalls. The long backbone of the mountain towers darkly over Patterdale and Glenridding and beckons the adventurer to explore its mysteries and its delights. From the west you trudge up unromantic slopes, looking down on a reservoir and perhaps buses and chemical containers grinding slowly over the pass, but from the Ullswater side the fell-walker can be sure of an interesting ascent, with fine, lifting views all around him. He can either go along the ridges or up through the hanging valleys between or he can switch from one to the other. Most people go up the ridges, and Striding Edge on a sunny Sunday afternoon can be rather like a seaside promenade. But the views are better than they are at any seaside and the interest is maintained to the very top where one is suddenly presented with a completely different set of views, embracing most of Lakeland. The summit may be dull but the views from it can be superlative.

Years ago the timid fought shy of Striding Edge but except in appalling weather it is difficult to see how anybody could fall over the side, other than by jumping off. People who don't like heights can avoid the actual rooftree but the average youngster of five or six will trip along without a thought. My dog has often done the round trip—up Striding Edge and down Swirrel —and he's supposed to be lazy and unenterprising. The young exploration group members who did the survey found out that Striding Edge was by far the most popular way up, and the straightforward descent to Wythburn the favoured way down. Swirrel Edge was the next popular route of descent, so that on the whole most people try to get the best out of the mountain by choosing the more adventurous ways. The mountain top investigators also found out a number of other things about some of Helvellyn's visitors. Only about two-thirds of them, for instance, had adequate clothing, foot-gear or equipment, many had neither maps nor guide-books and some, when questioned, did not even realize they were on the summit of Helvellyn. Several parties of young people were very poorly organized, and lost stragglers were always turning up. Many people, apparently, still don't know how to look after themselves in the hills—even on Helvellyn.

But I don't think I've ever been up Helvellyn without meeting somebody somewhere on the mountain and therein lies its value. It may be the tourists' mountain but no matter what the weather, you can go up there and find somebody else doing the same thing. You're never likely to be frightened, or lonely or even depressed up there, for Helvellyn, the 'sunrise mountain', is a genial giant and generally looks after his guests.

Dollywaggon Pike

Whenever I see or hear the name Dollywaggon Pike—and sometimes when I'm on the mountain—I think of a happy summer scene of fifty, or perhaps a hundred, years ago that, for me, smacks of the real Lakeland of long ago. Immediately, the name conjures up a picture of laughing children and jolly rustics bowling along in a wagonette to, say, Grasmere sports or it may be just to the May Queen festival. The children are wearing huge sun-bonnets tied up with blue ribbons, the day is very warm, and everybody is singing, or, at any rate, making merry. That's what a name can do for you—if you've a little imagination. I suppose 'waggon' is the principal association, while 'Dolly' suggests children. And Grasmere sports perhaps come to mind because I once went there in a four-in-hand.

But Dollywaggon Pike has nothing to do with waggons or children, although it's not very far from Grasmere. It is rather

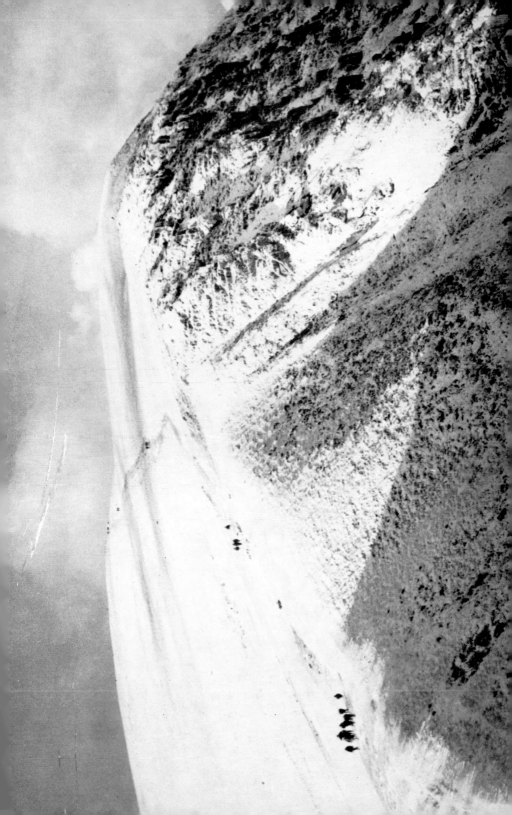

a dull feature of the Helvellyn range from one side, a fine, rocky mountain from the other but, surprisingly for a mountain so close to the trade routes, a relatively little-known peak. No doubt, it is crossed as often as any other mountain in Lakeland, but its actual summit is not often visited and its best side is almost unknown to the average walker. Everybody, you might say, knows Dollywaggon Pike but few know it really well.

A little way down its western flank lies Willie Wife Moor which I find just as fascinating a name as that of the peak, and with a somewhat similar association. Undoubtedly, the Willie Wife would be in the wagonette with the children—a fat, jolly, country woman with cheeks like red apples and a high-pitched voice you could hear down at Goody Bridge. How these steep, grassy slopes came to be so named I cannot say, but the name of the peak, I am credibly informed, almost certainly comes from Old Norse. Obviously, Dollywaggon is not a descriptive name but nevertheless it has, for me, some poetic charm, and sounds just as fine—in a different sort of way—as splendid mountain names like Blencathra, Glaramara and Seatallan.

That redoubtable traveller, Captain Joseph Budworth, perhaps the first man to go into the Lakeland hills for the fun of it, decided that Dollywaggon had been so named "in remembrance of some rustic fun", but this seems most unlikely. Possibly, the gallant captain had much the same picture as myself, but mountains don't seem to get named this way. Another interpretation is that the mountain was named after "Wagen", the servant of some Norse chieftain, but this explanation is not thought to be very reliable, either. The most probable origin of the name is from dolgr meaning 'fiend' or 'giant' in Old Norse and veginn meaning 'lifted'. And 'the lifted peak of the giant' sounds a pretty fair description of Dollywaggon, especially if you are looking at it from Grisedale on a day when the mists are swirling about its crags. "Quite the Troll's work," was Professor Collingwood's description.

It is unfortunate that the thousands of people who each year laboriously climb the Dollywaggon zigzags on their way from Grasmere to Helvellyn see little or nothing of the real mountain, which is mostly far round the corner to the right. Very few of them even bother to go on to the summit which is a little way above the well-trodden highway so that even on a crowded day in midsummer you can generally have this splendid viewpoint

9

Watson's Dodd from Smaithwaite

to yourself. A much better way up the mountain from Grisedale
Tarn is to avoid the zigzags, which were made for ponies anyway, and scramble up the fellside some distance to the right of
them. In this way you can at least look down into the gullies
which make up much of the real architecture of the mountain.

If you study these gullies from Grisedale or, better still,
from the fells on the opposite side of the valley, you will see how
impressively they cleave the crags and you will easily understand how they came to attract the attention of some of the men
who began the British sport of rock-climbing. The Abraham
brothers of Keswick—George, the elder, died in 1965 at the
age of ninety-three—made the first ascent of Dollywaggon
Gully as long ago as 1894, and three years later, Lieut.-Col.
H. Westmorland, then a boy of eleven or so, was exploring
the area with his father. On their way to the Tarn Crag and
Falcon Crag cliffs of Dollywaggon the two happened to meet a
most formidable climbing party which consisted of J. W.
Robinson of Lorton, Haskett Smith (who first climbed Napes
Needle), Ellis Carr and Geoffrey Hastings. These four had just
failed in an attempt on the 'big gully' on Dollywaggon which
today we call Chock Gully and it was not to be expected that
the youngster and his father could do better. But the following
year young Westmorland, again with his father, got about
twenty feet up the big pitch and then twelve years later, in
1910, was able to lead his two cousins in the first ascent of the
whole climb.

But fifty years before even the Abrahams there was climbing
activity of a sort in the valley, according to an old record—
perhaps the very first record of a 'climb' if you could call it that,
in the Lake District. It took place on 'the eagle's crag' in
Grisedale, which could be Eagle Crag, a little distance down
the valley where I myself was concerned in some exploration a
few years ago, or it might have been on one of the Dollywaggon
cliffs. The climbers were Edward Rose, a parson described as
"an experienced cragsman" and George Butler, later a Canon.
Matthew Arnold and A. H. Clough were also in the party,
although not on the climb. Half-way up the cliff a hold gave way
and Butler might have crashed on to the screes had his shooting
jacket not caught on a projecting corner. But he subsequently
extricated himself and surmounted the difficulty by hooking his
walking-stick, described as a Kendal hazel, on to a jutting rock
overhead. It can't have been much of a climb, since he had a
walking-stick with him, but even so nobody had ever written

about even this sort of a scramble in Lakeland before, to the best of my knowledge.

Today, these wild places are not very much better known than they were fifty years ago, which is an excellent thing. When the zigzags are crowded with pedestrians and the Helvellyn track a noisy highway you can still scramble about these rocky combes, even if you are no climber, and spend a quiet restful day. Due east of Dollywaggon summit and easily reached from Grisedale is Cock Cove, and, further to the north, the fine combe of Ruthwaite Cove. Tourists seldom go into these places but this is much the best side of the mountain, and the scramble from Ruthwaite Lodge and up The Tongue much the best way to the summit. Ruthwaite Cove, in particular, with its cascades, caves and crags is a wonderful place and near the head of the combe, just underneath the summit crags of Nethermost Pike, is Hard Tarn, a dark, little pool on a ledge of rock. Although this tarn can be seen from the Helvellyn ridge and also from Fairfield it is very rarely visited but the pool has considerable charm and character especially when lit by the morning sun.

Dollywaggon's principal sheet of water is, of course, Grisedale Tarn—a place with many real and fancied associations with the distant past, and a tarn that seems to reflect colours from the mountains and the sky to a greater degree than many other similar places. I particularly enjoy the colours in this tarn in the winter-time when it can sometimes seem a strangely exciting pool. They say that the hollow of Grisedale Tarn was formed by a huge glacier flowing down from Scafell, and you can see the glacial debris there. Just to the north of the tarn is the Brothers' Rock where Wordsworth parted from his brother John who was later drowned off Portland in 1805.

The western flank of Dollywaggon is its dull side, although Birkside Gill contains some fine cascades and waterfalls, and the route up Raise Beck from the top of Dunmail is a straightforward way to the summit. We used to carry skis up this way until we decided that the tussocky slopes of Willie Wife Moor, although often nicely plastered with snow, do not really lend themselves to good ski-ing. No, it is the eastern side of Dollywaggon that matters—a wild, tumbled mountainside, remote and secluded even when Striding Edge is thronged with people. A place, in bad weather, much more reminiscent of the lifted peak of the giant than of the happy children in the wagonette. Still, it's a pretty picture and will always be there when I think of Dollywaggon Pike.

Raise

Nearly all my memories of Raise are of winter days—short days of struggling in the snow against icy winds, days of mist and rain, occasional evenings picking our way in the darkness down the zigzags to the lights of Glenridding, but also many, many happy days of sunlight on glistening snows, with magnificent views over most of Lakeland. Mostly we have been on skis or carrying them wearily uphill, for this rather unimpressive hump in the Helvellyn range happens to carry more snow longer— at sufficiently convenient angles—than any other mountain in Lakeland. Winter-sports enthusiasts who may know no other Lake District fell go up Raise several times each winter for the pleasure of sliding down it on skis, and a few years ago their activities were facilitated by the provision of a diesel-driven ski-tow, designed to take out some of the hard work.

Few people would call Raise an especially shapely mountain nor even a peak of character but it has—in addition to its ski-ing potentialities—several features of interest which stamp it with some individuality. Its name, for instance, is unusual, and until the skiers discovered the place it must have been one of the least-known mountain names in the district. And even today the name is so little known outside the winter-sports world that if you told most people—even Lake District folk—you were going up Raise they would conclude you were referring to the road ascent of Dunmail. Even the knowledgeable fell walker might think you were referring to High Raise behind Langdale Pikes, while the lists of the principal mountains of Lakeland rarely, or never, mention Raise. Yet this rather sprawling mass of up-lifted land along one of the best-known mountain ranges in the district is, in fact, about the tenth highest peak in Lakeland, comfortably placed in order of seniority between Fairfield and Esk Pike.

Raise carries the Cumberland-Westmorland boundary along its rock-crowned summit, overlooks Sticks Pass, the second highest pass in Lakeland, and is scarred on its eastern slopes by the ruined remains of the former Glenridding lead mining industry. It has been said that the Romans could have been the first to dig for minerals on the lower spurs of the mountain and certainly there was mining there for hundreds of years. But now the adits have been sealed, most of the mine buildings pulled down and the spoil-heaps grassed over so that in years to come men might pass this way and not know that hereabouts was once an important Lakeland industry with its origins steeped in history. Curiously enough, the last work to be done in this ancient mine was not the winning of lead but the detonation, in the far depths of one of the shafts that almost tunnel under Ullswater, of a gunpowder charge, specifically arranged in connection with the important study of the effects of underground nuclear explosions. In its very last days, therefore, the old mine played its part in research into one of the world's most pressing problems.

On the eastern slopes of the mountain may be traced the line of the mile-long stone aqueduct or flue which formerly served the mine, and at its head there is the remains of the chimney, nowadays used as a shelter by walkers or skiers. There is some confusion over what might have been the exact use of this strange feature. Postlethwaite, the authority on mining in the Lake District, says that the whole mile of it was in fact a chimney, its purpose being the condensation and deposition of particles of ore thrown off by the smelting furnaces. Manholes were provided so that the chimney could be swept from time to time and the particles of ore reclaimed. Later authorities have questioned this explanation but most of the evidence seems to suggest that the 'chimney' or flue was originally an iron pipe laid in a stone-lined trench and later roughly removed, and that it terminated in the conventional chimney now in ruins.

Three stretches of standing water used to decorate the mountain, but since the bursting of the Keppel Cove Tarn dam in 1927 during exceptionally heavy rainfall and gales, this little lake underneath the wall of the Helvellyn range and due south of the summit of the mountain, has been dry. When the dam burst a great wall of water rushed down the Glenridding Beck, uprooting trees, carrying away a bridge and flooding houses and farms five or six feet deep. A tea hut, furniture, wireless sets, dead sheep and chests of meal are said to have been swept into the lake and washed across to the opposite shore. The other sheets of water were the rather ugly reservoir—now drained and even uglier—on the way up the Sticks Pass track, and the tiny tarn near the top of the pass. Otherwise, the mountain is largely featureless although there are the crags encircling Keppel Cove, the 'forest' of juniper at Stang End, the rock outcrop a little east of the summit that serves to identify the mountain in some views and, not least, the rocky summit itself. This last feature is worthy of note since the summit of Raise is the only one in the Helvellyn range that looks like a mountain top.

For generations, Raise was little more than a minor feature of the well-tracked walk across the Helvellyn range, part of the gateway of the popular Sticks Pass, and always a fine viewpoint, but since its 'discovery' by the skiers it has become almost hallowed ground. The Lake District Ski Club now have a hut on its shoulders on the 2,500-feet contour—one of the highest huts in Britain—and nearby is the ski-tow. Here, any winter weekend when there's snow about, you will find the skiers, mostly congregated around a steep snow-slope known to the initiated as Savage's Drift. This slope faces north-east, and this is the corner of the mountain that retains snow longer than almost any other spot in Lakeland. One year, for instance, I was ski-ing there in glorious sunshine on the last Sunday in April and I've no doubt you could have skied there that year in May.

The wind can be very fierce and cold on this side of the mountain and I remember once struggling there in skis on ice in the teeth of a savage wind with a companion who had just come back from nine months in South Georgia which has as bad a climate as anywhere in the world. Between gusts I observed to my companion through chattering teeth: "I suppose this sort of weather's nothing to you," but he assured me that his expedition had never ventured outside its tents when the weather had been as bad as it was that day on Raise. A few minutes later I happened to knock over a flask of hot coffee on to the snow. In a second—or so it seemed—it had frozen solid.

But the weather is by no means always like this on Raise and I can think of many splendid winter days up there when you could sit about in the sunshine in shirt-sleeves admiring, between twisting runs down the steep ribbons of snow, the evening light on the High Street range or, from higher up on the summit rocks, the Keswick hills or the sun dipping down behind the Derwent Fells. I remember, one winter day, watching a herd of red deer—the biggest I'd seen outside Scotland—come chasing down from the summit towards Stang and then disappearing among the juniper above Glenridding Beck. And certainly this shy, perhaps undistinguished, mountain has many days like this to offer every winter, and they are all well worth the slog up the zigzags from the mines or by way of Fisher Gill from Thirlspot on the Keswick road.

And when you next go up Raise for the snows think of the

very earliest 'skiers' on the mountain. These were the miners of a hundred, two hundred or three hundred years ago who, during the winter months, used to live up there in crude huts and when they yearned for a bit of village life used to slither down the snows to the Glenridding hostelries with barrel staves or bits of planking strapped to their feet. Which was long, long before the sport of ski-ing came to the Lake District or even to Europe.

The Dodds

There was one day during the glorious Indian Summer of 1964 when the Lake District hills looked as sharp against the blue sky as if they'd been cut out of coloured cardboard, when the smoke rose straight from the chimney-pots in the valley and you could almost hear the insects talking. I was alone on the Dodds, those little-visited hills to the north of the Helvellyn range, and not only saw nobody all day but hardly heard a sound either. Three miles away coach-loads of tourists were noisily exploring Aira Force—I saw some of them later—and I've no doubt there were processions going over Helvellyn, but nobody else had thought it worthwhile going up into these lonely little fells.

If you study the 1-inch to the mile Ordnance Survey map of Lakeland you will see that the area of the Dodds seems to contain fewer crags, woods, tarns and other features than almost anywhere else—except perhaps the remote country at the 'back o' Skiddaw'. The map, too, looks oddly bare of printing in this area so that the walker could gain the impression that the Dodds are remarkably lacking in interest and should be avoided at all costs. But this is hardly true. Admitted, it's all very easy walking with nothing very dramatic or exciting around you. No crags, except some down by the road; no tarns to speak of—just a couple of pools; almost no sculpturing of the mountain sides; little heather and bracken—just miles of grass. However, at least there's the loneliness, the quietude, the splendid springy turf, and the feeling that you can look out, around the whole compass, at the bigger mountains as if from some upland promenade. And in these days of crowded and noisy mountain tops, cairns every hundred yards or so, and litter never very far away, these can be important considerations. Indeed, a lone tour of the Dodds—particularly in winter with crisp snows and Alpine views—can be more rewarding than a walk up Gable or Scafell on a day when everybody else seems to be doing the same thing.

Perhaps the Dodds are the least-known bit of Lakeland. Certainly I've never seen anybody up there—except when we've been ski-ing on Stybarrow Dodd—and on my last visit in late summer I met nobody from leaving Dockray about eleven o'clock in the morning until my return there six hours later. I went from Dockray along the old coach-road that contours the skirts of these northern fells and eventually brings you to Threlkeld. It was a bright morning with remarkably clear views and for once I heartily disagreed with the late Mr. Baddeley— one of the very few guide-writers to bother to go this way—who considered this old road "dull and monotonous". Straight in front, across the slopes of Threlkeld Common rose the sharp, serrated ridges of Blencathra and I have rarely seen them looking so fine. From three or four miles away I seemed to be able to pick out every boulder and bilberry patch.

One of the rewards of traversing this old road, if you chose this sort of a morning, is the sudden view, as you come round the shoulder of Clough Head, of the whole of the Borrowdale and Buttermere fells, with Keswick and Derwentwater nestling below and Skiddaw soaring impressively to the right. On that morning I watched the smoke rising straight from the Keswick chimneys and, above the haze, a score of friendly peaks basking in the sunlight.

It was really, I remember, a day out for my dog Sambo who needed the exercise, and our route went over the tops of Clough Head, Great Dodd, Watson's Dodd, Stybarrow Dodd and then back over Hart Side and Birkett Fell. There's so much grass on these fells that you come upon the cluster of rocks that make up the staging post of Calfhow Pike with some relief. It is strange how little we know about these fells. Why, for instance, are they called Dodds (the Ordnance Survey prefers Dod), who was Watson of Watson's Dodd—perhaps the coach-travellers of last century knew—and why, until it was decided to call one top Birkett Fell in honour of the late Lord Birkett, was it called, quite simply, Nameless Fell? And what is the strange ditch across the summit of Hart Side, and what is the story behind Fisher's Wife Rake on Clough Head, and why is Jim's Fold so called?

These fells can be very dry, with only little pools on Stybarrow and Watson's to welcome the thirsty traveller, but there are fine waterfalls lower down the western slopes in Stanah Gill, Fisher Gill and Mill Gill. And although the Dodds are remarkably devoid of rock, there is, low down on Watson's at the entrance to the Vale of St. John, the wonderfully steep Castle Rock of Triermain. To reach this crag from the road you cross Manchester's water-race and then decide whether you want to climb on the south crag where the climbs are rather easier or on the north crag where nearly all of them are remarkably steep and even overhanging in places. The first man to climb the north crag was Jim Birkett, the Little Langdale quarryman and one of the pioneers of Lakeland climbing, who, in 1939, made Overhanging Bastion which follows the remarkable gangway going steeply up the crag. If you are unlucky enough to fall off this gangway you are likely to be suspended, spinning on your rope in mid-air, since the crag is undercut. Since that day much harder climbs have been done on this vertical crag—some of them among the hardest in Lakeland—but to do them you have to run the risk of being watched by incredulous spectators from the roadside, and this can be unnerving.

Low down on Clough Head there are Wanthwaite Crags and Bram Crag and, in between, the ravine of Sandbed Gill so called because the waterfalls disappear into a bed of sand by the side of the road. Not many years ago this gill was climbed by a Lakeland mountaineer and since there was no known record of any other ascent it was recorded as a probable first ascent. Two or three of us had since been there on several occasions, the climb having some botanical and ornithological, if little climbing, interest and it was several years later that it was discovered that the first ascent had, in fact, been made by the ubiquitous Abraham brothers of Keswick, as long ago as 1890.

The other excitements of the Dodds have to be sought out but you will probably content yourself with the loneliness, the peace and the views. The summit of Clough Head, for instance, must be one of the finest viewpoints in Lakeland. To the south-east the view is blocked by the bulk of Great Dodd but elsewhere, all round the compass, you can see dozens of mountains from the Coniston Fells to High Street. I came down at the end of my walk, to Dowthwaitehead, the remote hamlet where they probably hardly see the sun in winter and the snow can lie for months. They say that both the yellow and the blue mountain pansy grow around there but I have never spotted them.

Some day I would like to do the route on skis—it should make a wonderful expedition—but in summer-time I think you should pick your day for the Dodds. On the wrong sort of day and if you are not in the right mood they could, perhaps, be rather dreary.

But if you are a little lazy, or want to be alone, or are anxious to see the district from a new angle, try the Dodds on a bright April morning and capture the contentment that the loneliest fells in Lakeland can give you.

9

ABOVE THE DERWENT

(Around Borrowdale)

Glaramara

IT is a strange thing but I have never thought of Glaramara as a mountain, still less as a peak. To me it has always been a fell—a long, straggling line of fell with not much mountain shape and hardly any beginning or end. It is not very obvious where it all starts and there are so many summits and bumps along the ridge that it is not always clear whether or not one has arrived on the top and, sometimes, whether one is going up or down. Indeed, people rarely talk of going 'up' Glaramara but more often of going 'over' or 'along' the fell.

But this is not to suggest that Glaramara—the name is Celtic, not Norse—is anything but a most splendid section of upland Lakeland. For me, it is a fell with one of the loveliest names in the district, full of interest with surprises around every corner, a magnificent viewpoint, and a place of great charm and individuality. And the little tarns scattered along its undulating summit ridge are among the finest in the National Park.

Like so many other fells of character Glaramara has no clearly recognizable shape. Although it is an isolated mass occupying almost the whole of the area between Grains Gill and Langstrath Beck it rarely obtrudes on the skyline, and often its switchback ridge seems to melt, almost shyly, into adjoining, and more impressive, contours. Many people identifying Lakeland peaks from a distant viewpoint might fail completely to pick out the fell at all or, having sorted out the others, declare: "So that lump over there must be Glaramara."

Fortunately for those of us who prefer our mountains to be quiet and lonely, Glaramara is not a particularly popular fell. It was, indeed, almost trackless until a holiday guest-house was established near the Seatoller road end some years ago, borrowing 'Glaramara' as its name. Since then the fell has been much more in use and there is now a pleasant path along the ridge, with other tracks wending upwards from the valley. But Glaramara is still less spoiled by mass tourism, litter, cairns and other signs of over-popularity than many less worthy places.

One reason for this comparative neglect might be that Glaramara has come to be regarded as a nasty place in mist or bad weather—an impression worth encouraging. Certainly, it can be easy in difficult conditions to get lost on Glaramara and, even with a compass and the ability to use it, particular care is sometimes required. The hummocky nature of the ground, the crags on either side of the ridge, some bad stretches of bog and the deeply cut gills can make the steering of a compass-course a tricky problem. I remember once going across the fell from the remote little pool of Tarn at Leaves to Stockley Bridge in very bad weather and although I thought I knew the ground fairly well it was necessary in more than one place to retrace my steps and work out a better route. The fell must be one of the best places in the district for trying out young people in the use of map and compass.

Glaramara was probably the original name for the rocky summit of the fell but it has come to be applied to the whole ridge from Thornythwaite to Allen Crags, including Thornythwaite Fell itself, while Rosthwaite Fell might also be included in the massif by the less finicky visitor. In effect, Glaramara is almost the north-eastern spur of the Scafells since there is only a shallow drop at the end of the long ridge to the summit of Esk Hause at nearly 2,500 feet before the steep surge up to Great End. But the character of Glaramara, well-wooded on its lower slopes and rounded, tumbled and sprawling along its backbone, has little in common with the Scafells. There is no pleasanter way to the highest land in England than along the Glaramara switchback but when you look across the Hause from the top of Allen Crags you are looking at a different, wilder country.

Perhaps Glaramara's most prominent feature is the wonderful hanging valley of Comb Gill—Combe Gill to some people—which faces northwards up the length of Borrowdale but is surprisingly little-visited by tourists, although well known to climbers. The valley contains many rock routes, notably on Raven Crag which faces east and is split by the fine gully which first attracted climbers into the combe about seventy years ago and, facing this crag, is the remarkable mass of rock known as Doves' Nest caves. There is no other place quite like this in the Lake District. A great buttress of rock slipped down the fellside hundreds or thousands of years ago but instead of crashing into scree at the foot of the cliff its fall was arrested, and it now leans back against the parent crag, leaving great fissures and holes underneath and at the back. These are the caves and you will need candles or head-lamps together with the necessary climbing skill to explore them. The game is a mixture of pot-holing and climbing—a great place to bring adventurous children on a wet day, with some rewarding, quite exciting routes. Some of the climbs, after you have emerged from the depths, continue on the outside walls above so that you can be dry and warm in the darkness one minute, and cold and wet in the upper air a few moments later. They used to say that these caves were the last retreat in Lakeland of the wolves. If so, they chose an ideal place as their lair.

Glaramara is more often reached from Comb Gill than from other directions, apart, perhaps, from the ridge route from Allen Crags, but for the climber there is an interesting approach from Langstrath by way of Cam Crag Ridge, which is about 700 feet high and leads to the top of Rosthwaite Fell and thence on to Glaramara. It is a very easy route for the climber, but not for the walker. This ridge is, in effect, the ascent of a mountainside where the hands are required as well as the feet—a circumstance fairly unusual in Lakeland.

One of the principal glories of Glaramara is the walk to Allen Crags along the broad grassy ridge, with the wonderful succession of lovely tarns, and the magnificent views over most of Lakeland which are continually provided. Only one tarn, High House Tarn, is named on the 1-inch Ordnance Survey map but there must be at least six of them between the summit and Allen Crags and almost all of them are gems. If you approach the ridge from Comb Gill there are one or two small tarns near the col but the finest collection is beyond Pinnacle Bield, the largest of them being High House Tarn. There are trout in this delightful tarn which may be used as the foreground for a graphic picture of Pike o' Stickle, two or three miles away to the south-east. A few hundred yards away to the south lies Lincomb Tarn which is a real jewel. It is cradled in steep, little crags that make a sort of gateway for exciting views of the surrounding fells. There are few finer mountain tarns in the whole of Lakeland than this one, although all the others along this ridge are worth visiting. But you must keep your eyes open to spot them all for some are hidden round the back of little crags. And around the pools you find boggy ground, flecked here and there, in season, with marsh grass, stonecrops and saxifrages, with perhaps bog asphodel and cotton grass, and an occasional clump of the lovely Grass of Parnassus. All the way along this ridge the views are magnificent, for Glaramara is not overshadowed by any other mountain, and the walk southwards towards the highest land in England is probably the special glory of the fell. Perhaps the best view of all, however, is that from the summit northwards along the curve of Borrowdale with the wooded valley in the middle distance and then, beyond, Derwentwater and its islands, and, in the distance, the proud shape of Skiddaw and his attendant fells.

Glaramara will always be a favourite fell of mine for it is a place quite unlike anywhere else in Lakeland, full of quiet beauty and individuality and with plenty of scope for mild adventuring. I remember many sunny summer evenings spent down on the skirts of the fell at Thornythwaite Farm. Several times I have watched the sun going down over the hills and seen the great mass of Glaramara slowly turn from what seemed a huge lump of gold into the deepest purple. A shy fell, perhaps, but although not particularly photogenic from a distance in ordinary lighting it can be one of the most rewarding places in Lakeland to visit with a colour camera. For Glaramara is a place to examine closely—the tarns, the crags and the caves—or to look out from. I only hope it will always remain a fell for the connoisseur and never be ruined by the hordes.

Catbells

Some people wouldn't call Catbells a real mountain for it falls short of 1,500 feet and is regularly ascended by young children in gym-shoes and old men with walking-sticks. But it is shaped like a mountain, and for all its modest height commands one of the most pleasantly airy views in the district. And though it may be the most pedestrian little fell in Lakeland, it is also the start of a particularly rewarding round of the tops. Most of all, however, it is a family hill—a place for toddlers and grandfathers; a place for early morning exercise or for a breath of fresh air on a still summer's evening; a place for shy lovers, picnic parties, and yelping dogs. You'll find them all on top in the crowded holiday months.

It was, I remember, my daughter's first 'mountain'—ticked off at the age of two and a half, although I'm quite sure many younger fell-walkers have reached the top. For although the paths may be steep in places, there are plenty of them and little danger, provided you don't fall down one of the mine-shafts.

Catbells is a lovely little hill, both to look at and to look from—a smoothly sculptured cone, pushed up between the glories of Borrowdale and the splendid architecture of the Newlands fells, and sufficiently far from Keswick for seeing only the very best in Lakeland's northern capital. From the rocky but cairnless summit Keswick looks a fairy town in a magic landscape, and the lake, ringed with wooded fells and dotted with islands and boats, an enchanting place for youthful adventure.

Indeed, this little mountain has always seemed, for me, to have its own special magical quality. You could hardly think of a prettier name for a child's mountain—although it is probably derived from Cat Bield, the shelter of the wild cat—and at least two Lakeland writers have peopled the little fell with romantic characters. It was here, for instance, that Beatrix Potter's Mrs. Tiggy-Winkle had some of her adventures, finally disappearing into a door somewhere in the Vale of Newlands. And more than one of Sir Hugh Walpole's heroes strode these grassy slopes or ran up through the bracken to watch the sun setting behind Grasmoor.

Walpole himself had his home on the slopes of Catbells, looking out over Derwentwater. He had found Brackenburn during a house-hunting expedition in Lakeland in November, 1923, and described it: "A little paradise on Catbells. Running stream, garden, lawn, daffodils, squirrels, music room, garage, four bedrooms and a bath." One look at the place had been enough and he bought it at the price asked without even seeking professional advice. He lived on or off at Brackenburn for seventeen years—but never longer than five weeks at a stretch. Each morning he would cross the lawn after breakfast to his desk in his big library over the garage, take up his pen and write quickly, sometimes at the rate of more than a thousand words an hour. Sometimes he was describing scenes he could see from his windows and he made one of his characters, Adam Paris, live in a cottage on Catbells so that inspiration could come easily.

One afternoon at Brackenburn when he was out walking on

the slopes of Catbells with his dog he came for the first time on a jutting promontory of grass and rock high above his house, and as he sat there, drinking in the panorama of lakes and mountains, he thought he saw his whole life stretched out ahead of him. He often returned to this spot and after his death a friend, in fulfilment of a promise, caused a stone seat to be built there so that others could share the author's delight.

From the airy summit of Catbells you can either drop down to Hawse End, Brandlehow or Newlands or you can continue along the ridge to Maiden Moor and thence up and down the skyline until you reach Buttermere, or circle over Hindscarth or Robinson and back to Keswick. The ridge provides one of the pleasantest upland walks in Lakeland, with beauty all around and hardly a jarring note. You start with Derwentwater low down on your left and its tiny craft looking like matches floating in a pool, the length of lovely Borrowdale straight ahead and the green trough of Newlands where the German miners worked below the craggy slopes to the right.

This is hill-walking at its best—springy turf, often a steady breeze to keep the cloud patterns nicely changing, superb views all around, and a wonderful feeling, despite the modest height, of being on top of everything. Grisedale Pike and the switchback skyline of the Coledale fells are far enough away not to over-power, while the Scafell giants to the south remain hidden by the rising ground ahead so that you are on top of your own little world, and can remain so, on the spine of the mountains, all the way back to Keswick.

At one point on the ridge, not long after leaving the summit of Catbells you are standing immediately above the old Gold-scope mine in Newlands where the Germans began winning copper, as well as silver and gold, four hundred years ago. Later the Dutch worked the mine which was afterwards aban-doned, but it was reopened last century and again during the First World War. And there are other old mines on Catbells itself—the Old Brandley Mine to the north of the summit, Brandlehow Mine on the lake shore, and Yewthwaite Mine above Little Town. Walkers should take care in the neighbour-hood of these open shafts which have caused at least one death in recent years.

Besides its literary associations Catbells has its connections with the outdoor movements. Brandelhow Park on the side of the fell lapped by the lake waters was the first property in the Lake District to be acquired by the National Trust nearly

Great End and Sprinkling Tarn

seventy years ago, while on the Hawse End ascent there is a memorial tablet set in the rock to the memory of Mr. T. A. Leonard, a great pioneer of open-air organizations. Canon Rawnsley, Vicar of Crosthwaite just three miles away, was one of the founders of the National Trust and through his efforts and the efforts of Miss Octavia Hill the sum of £6,500 was raised in six months to save Brandelhow Park from falling into the hands of the builders.

The last time I was on Catbells was immediately after a day of great floods in Lakeland. From the top the county of Cumberland looked sparkling, well-washed and colourful while Derwentwater had swollen almost as far as Grange and the new bridge across the Derwent was in the middle of the lake. We strolled along the ridge in the morning sunshine—Maiden Moor, Eel Crags, Dale Head and then back along Hindscarth after a couple of climbs on one of the crags. It was, I remember, a perfect evening when we came down into Newlands and along the shadowed lanes back to the foot of Catbells. A farmer was taking back his cows after milking and somewhere near Gill Bank a foxhound, lost perhaps from a hunt, was padding his lone way home. It was warm even after the sun went down and as we passed a cattle trough in the lane we dropped the dog in so that he could cool off, and then headed past hedgerows of birch, hawthorn and rowan in the sweet smelling dusk for the night life of Keswick.

Those are the sort of memories I have of Catbells—of peaceful summer evenings on and around a children's playground, of a hill set in the middle of the warmest and most colourful scenery in England. And I like to think that when I get too old and decrepit to climb rocks or ski or walk up proper mountains, I will still be able to drag myself up little Catbells and look out over the immeasurably beautiful scene of lakes, islands, woods, hills and valleys, with the happy town of Keswick most fortunately set down right in the middle of it all.

High Spy

Not many people know High Spy—the name, that is, not the mountain. They know High Street, High Raise, High Stile and the rest but not High Spy. Baddeley never mentioned it, nor Palmer nor Symonds and yet High Spy overlooks what is probably the best bit of Borrowdale, perhaps the most popular valley in the whole of Lakeland.

10

The Grasmoor range and Buttermere

When I knew the mountain well, many years ago, I knew it as Scawdel Fell and we used to refer to it as, simply, "Scawd'l". Sometimes we called it Lobstone Band but it was only when we started poring over maps that we discovered its real name was High Spy. But they certainly don't call it High Spy in Borrowdale. The quarrymen used to call the whole fell west of Rosthwaite "Scawd'l" and the map calls Goat Crag behind Castle Crag, Low Scawdel and the lump of land above Seatoller, High Scawdel. And since High Scawdel is lower than High Spy it is all very confusing. My conclusion is that High Spy is merely the name of the summit—a good name for a perch that looks down the precipices of Eel Crags—and that Lobstone Band is the name of the shoulder that slants down to Borrowdale. Some maps call the mountain Eel Crags but this is really the name of the mile-long precipice overlooking the upper reaches of Newlands. This name has nothing to do with eels but is a contraction of e'il or evil, expressing the rather dark, menacing nature of these cliffs—until you get to know them well.

High Spy is really a fine, bulky mountain with much more than its fair share of crag, but it looks disappointingly shapeless from the valley. You've got to swarm up it from two or three sides and walk along its fine ridge to appreciate its worth. Eel Crags is one of the biggest stretches of cliff in Lakeland but it was almost completely ignored by rock-climbers until 1948. Newlands Gully had been climbed by the Woodhouse brothers as long ago as 1913 and a second route nearby was put up ten years later but nobody bothered to explore the long line of broken buttresses until after the Second World War. I remember once asking Jim Birkett, the well-known Lakeland climber from Little Langdale, whether he thought the crags worth exploring and he told me he'd had a look at them but they were too shattered and uninteresting to bother about. But a few years later about a score of good routes were put up, and the crag is a popular place nowadays with climbers who want to get away from the well-worn routes on the major cliffs.

I remember once having rather a painful experience in Newlands Gully. Two of us were climbing it, pitch about, when my friend who was leading happened to dislodge a rock which crashed down on to my head. Fortunately, I was wearing a woollen cap with a bobble on it which absorbed some of the blow but all the same it felt like being crushed by a falling sideboard. For a moment or two I felt a little groggy and my friend shouted down, "Tie yourself on in case you faint." And

I was about to comply with his suggestion when he, most inconsiderately, sent down a second chunk of rock. This time, however, I saw it coming and managed to deflect it with one arm which felt as if it had been under a steam-roller for some time afterwards. Anyway, I recovered and when it came my turn to lead scrambled up out of the place as quickly as I could lest I should get winged a third time. There was no serious damage but I was sore for a day or two and for a long time treated Eel Crags with great suspicion.

The crag has four main buttresses, named, respectively, as you approach the cliffs from Braithwaite: Grey Buttress, Red Crag, Waterfall Buttress and Miners' Crag. The last-named is the best crag, the first-named has perhaps the best rock, the second the worst and the third, the easiest. All the crags on Red Crag have Soviet-sounding names like October Slab, Cossack Crack and Kremlin Groove and most of them are fairly hard. Miners' Crag is, of course, named after the miners—the German miners who worked the Newlands Valley for copper and also found a little gold and silver. Goldscope, the name of this part of the valley, has probably nothing to do with the discovery of gold there, but is said to be a corruption of Gott's gab or God's gift—the name given by the Germans when they first struck the ore.

On the other side of the mountain is Goat Crag, pioneered as a climbing ground by the late Mr. Bentley Beetham, and also the well-known Castle Crag where he also started exploration. But, as he recorded, "the much-frequented tourist route passes its base and results in an audience below and a shower of scree from above from would-be spectators there, so I gave up making climbs."

Castle Crag is one of the tourist attractions of Lakeland—a thickly wooded pyramid of rock stuck in the jaws of the dale, riddled with quarry holes, strewn with scree slopes and spoil dumps but with a splendid view from the top. Here in a cave during the summer months lived Millican Dalton, the self-styled "Professor of Adventure" we used often to meet in Borrowdale in the old days. He made tents and rucksacks, took people on climbing trips to the Alps, acted as a guide for the more popular Lake District climbs, sailed a raft on Derwentwater, lived in the open and died just after the war at the age of eighty. I remember he used a battered old bicycle on which he slung most of his worldly possessions. He was a lovable old character and you can still see his lettering at the entrance to the cave: "Don't waste words: jump to conclusions." The crag was given to the National Trust in 1920 by Sir William Hamer and his family in memory of his son John, killed in the First World War. And nearly twenty years later Lady Hamer gave forty-six acres on the lower slopes as a memorial to Sir William.

Further round the mountain are more crags—Nitting Haws (a climb known as The Knitting Needle is nearby) and Blea Crag—so that most of the fell apart from the slope dropping down to the quarry track is encircled by rock. The track to the Rigg Head quarries from Rosthwaite is interesting if you care to explore the old workings and you come out on the moor, hard by Dale Head Tarn.

High Spy is volcanic rock and vegetation grows lush in summer-time in the combes between the crags. Few people, apart from climbers, explore the sides of the fell, the only traffic being along the top and up the Rigg Head track, but it is a mountain with deep roots in the past and a fascination for those willing to step aside from the busy valley road and do some probing. High Spy, plumb in the centre of the very best of Lakeland, deserves to be better known.

Great End

Only at dawn do the first, thin shafts of sunlight gild the edges of the crags of Great End and perhaps peep for a moment into the dark gullies, but then the sunshine slides round the back of the mountain and for the rest of the day the precipice remains shadowed and cold. This is the impression most of us have of Great End—a dark, rather forbidding, mountain wall overlooking the Esk Hause track. We know where it is but not very many of us bother to explore the place.

Great End suffers or gains—according to how you look at these things—from being a one-sided mountain and from being just off the route to the biggest peaks in England. Almost everything that Great End has to offer is placed in its north-facing window so that anybody approaching the highest land in the country from the north can see the dark shattered crag and its gullies. Even the motorist in Borrowdale—provided he knows where to look—can pick out Great End. But this is all that most people know of Great End—the sight of a dark crag on the way to Scafell Pike. Very few people indeed on this favourite pilgrimage turn aside from the well-worn track to walk the few hundred yards to the top of Great End, one of the most splendid viewpoints in Lakeland. The gullies open below your feet and at their foot is the jewel of Sprinkling Tarn, which at least one writer has found the most completely satisfying pool in the fell country. Beyond stretches the length of Borrowdale, with its fells and woods and fields, and then Derwentwater with Skiddaw behind. Almost certainly you will have this view to yourself. I don't think I've ever met anybody on the top of Great End.

The mountain is well named, for it is the splendid finish of the Scafell massif, which keeps above 2,500 feet for more than two miles. But on the edge of the highest ridge in the country, the plateau suddenly drops a thousand feet to the shelf that holds Sprinkling Tarn, and this giant step is Great End. The fact that the end of the ridge also has a summit and is a mountain in its own right seems almost incidental.

I have a feeling that Great End is even less known today than it used to be. Thirty years ago we used to go climbing in winter-time in the snow and ice-filled gullies of Great End because this was the only place we knew for winter mountaineering. Often in February or March—and occasionally even later—the gullies would be packed with hard snow steepening into ice in places, when you would have said at a glance that all the snow had disappeared from the hills. In summer-time the gullies made very uninteresting climbs but in winter they came into their own. This was where many of us learned the use of ice-axes and many climbers who have made big ascents in the Himalaya and elsewhere had their early training in step-cutting in the shadowed gullies of Great End. Winter-time thirty years ago meant Cust's, Central or South-East—the gullies of Great End —whereas today it means ski-ing, or, if climbing is preferred, it might be more ambitious gullies elsewhere in Lakeland or, more likely, in Scotland.

For the Great End gullies seem almost old-fashioned today, smacking of mountaineers in Norfolk jackets and large nailed boots. Haskett Smith climbed both Central and South-East more than eighty years ago, in each case alone, but I have no record of when Cust's, which is no more than a scramble, was first climbed. The average careful fell-walker would have no difficulty in summer-time with Cust's, high up towards the right of the crag and identified by a jammed boulder, but the other two main gullies, although disappointing as rock climbs, are not for the inexperienced tourist, either in summer or winter. My principal memories of Great End are of hauling myself out of one or other of these gullies in winter-time and enjoying the wonderful transition from the cold shadows to sunlit snows and splendid winter views over half of Lakeland. Often we have watched the sunset from Great End and then raced down the fellside to get back to Borrowdale or Wasdale before the darkness.

One of the ways up Great End is over The Band which is separated from the main mass of the mountain by the fine ravine of Skew Gill—a scramble in summer-time and an interesting route to the crag when snow-filled in winter. Beyond Skew Gill there is a broad shelf lying below the crags that lead to the summit ridge and several lovely little tarns lie in pockets on the shattered fellside. The only one of these pools to bear a name is Lambfoot Dub, and if you look closely you'll see that it is indeed shaped something like a lamb's foot. It lies below the pointed peak of Long Pike, and sits neatly above the drop down into the waterfalls of Greta Gill. This little tarn, perched among some of the wildest country in England and just above the Corridor Route to Scafell Pike which Heaton Cooper has called "the most dramatic mile in Lakeland", is a wonderful place for a summer's evening. All around are great crags and impressive ravines and just across the valley Great Gable rises bold against the sky. It is only a small tarn, shallow, filled with sparkling clear water and fringed with mountain grasses, but there are a few connoisseurs who consider it one of the mountain jewels of Lakeland.

Great End is one of the highest mountains in Lakeland, falling short of the magic three thousand feet by only sixteen feet but is hardly even mentioned in the guide-books. My old Ward Lock makes no reference to it whatsoever, although Wainwright finds it a worthy mountain. Thousands pass it every summer on their way up or down Esk Hause without giving it much more than a glance and most of the Scafell Pike traffic ignores it. And yet if you make the lovely approach to the Scafells by way of Grains Gill, Great End is in front of you all the way, increasingly dominating the view—much too impressive a mountain to be slighted.

Great End has nothing much to offer besides its fine crag and the recesses of Skew Gill—no spiky summit or hanging valleys or great ridges, just broken rock and scree and plenty of wild scenery in the very heart of mountain Lakeland. Go there on a winter's day with snow plastering the crag and perhaps mist encircling the mountain and you'll get the real atmosphere of Great End—aloof, unsmiling, but easily won and very well worth cultivating.

10

SHORT DAYS FROM STAIR

(Some North-west Hills)

Grasmoor

You can see Grasmoor from heights all over Lakeland—a lordly, sprawling hump at the end of a hummocky ridge—and from close at hand the mountain looks even better than it really is. Grasmoor may not come within my ten favourite mountains but I'm bound to admit that the view of its western flank from some places in Buttermere is one of the most impressive sights of bulk and steepness to be seen from any Lakeland main road. Far more dramatic, for instance, than the sight of Helvellyn from Dunmail, or Skiddaw from Keswick, or even the Scafells from the west.

Some people may agree that Grasmoor, with its acres of smoothly sloping turf, can be a dull mountain in places but, using your imagination quite a lot and choosing the right day, you *could* compare its great wall of broken crags towering over Crummock Water with the way the North Wall of the Eiger dominates Lauterbrunnen and the Grindelwald valley. Please don't misunderstand me. The Eiger wall is three times as high, nearly twice as steep, and an exceptionally formidable ascent compared with the rather boring scramble up the crumbling rock of Grasmoor End, but there *is* a certain similarity if you care to seek it out—especially under intimidating weather conditions. Seen from Lanthwaite Green the dark western wall of Grasmoor completely dwarfs the farms at its foot, and man-made things take on humble proportions against the towering rock and scree. Not far from the foot of the wall the picnickers and campers

stake their claims in summer-time and sometimes, perhaps, these
visitors, comfortably settled-in near Cinderdale Beck, look up
with apprehension at the rocky face and wonder whether they are
really safe from falling chunks of it. But there is really no
danger, for any loose rock prised away by the winter ice would
come to rest on the screes long before reaching the meadows.
And there is no fear of climbers dislodging pieces of rock, for
they don't bother to go there. Grasmoor End may look impressive but the face only yields two gully climbs of moderate
difficulty which are hardly worth seeking out when there are so
many much better things to climb a mile or two further up the
valley. There is another fine looking crag on the mountain—the
cirque of Dove Crags which drop away to the north from the
summit—but here the rock is far from sound and although one
or two of the gullies have been climbed the place is normally
avoided by climbers nowadays.

No, Grasmoor is a walker's mountain—one of the easiest in
the district to ascend if you go up from round 'the back' or
along the ridge—a remarkably fine viewpoint. And it can also
provide an interesting day for the botanist.

The name itself is misleading but, at a glance, surprisingly
accurate. Grasmoor really looks like a vast grassy moorland,
especially when you get on top, but the name has no more to do
with grass than has the name Grasmere. The derivation of the
'gras' comes from 'grise' (the wild boar) and you will find the
same root in place-names like Grisedale and Grizebeck. But it
is remarkable how many of the earlier guide-book writers got
the wrong name, and you will even find W. G. Collingwood
and W. T. Palmer spelling the mountain 'Grassmoor', not to
mention Ward, Lock and Co. Ltd. Of course, M. J. B. Baddeley
got it right and also guessed at the derivation, but then he
rarely got his facts wrong.

So the name Grasmoor has nothing to do with a grassy moorland, but although many of us might have known this for as long
as we can remember we still think of the mountain in this way—
I know I do. And, apart from its craggy western end and the
northern circle of Dove Crags, it is a much grassier mountain
than most others in Lakeland, besides being exceptionally well
clothed with flowers and shrubs. Indeed, I have been told by one
authority that the mountain probably grows more flora than
any other in the district, and I can certainly speak of the lushness
of its turf, the variety of its mountain flowers and the delicious
abundance of its bilberries. In season, you can walk across the

mountain and feel you are strolling through a mile-long rock garden. I dare say, if you tried hard enough, you could find forty or fifty plants in just one corner. Almost anything, it seems, can grow on Grasmoor, but not the red alpine catchfly, Lakeland's rarest plant. To find this you have to cross Gasgale Beck and scramble up the steep front of Hobcarton Crag, more than a mile away.

I suppose one reason for the abundance of its flora is the Skiddaw slate of which Grasmoor and many of the surrounding fells are made. This ancient rock breaks up into friable scree and brings about the gently swelling shapes of these north-west mountain slopes. The southern face of the long ridge that starts at Causey Pike and finishes on Grasmoor has a reddish tinge quite different from most other Lakeland fells, and the switch-back nature of this range seems completely characteristic and a very satisfying shape to study from across the valleys. Mostly, I like to see Grasmoor in the evening when the westering sun glows on the reddish screes and you can pick out the heather and the juniper among the crags.

You can run down off Grasmoor into Buttermere on some of the most perfect scree in the district and this can be the reward-ing end of a good day exploring the mountain. Apart from the plant life the principal feature of the summit plateau is the splendid view and the Dove Crags escarpment. Here is a grassy basin encircled by steep crags, and the combe looks as if it ought to contain a tarn. But there is no sign of there ever having been one here and no tarn that I can remember on the mountain. A few pleasant waterfalls in Cinderdale Beck but no pools—only the long length of Crummock Water washing the mountain's western skirts.

From the summit you see the receding ridges of High Stile and Red Pike, Great Gable, Kirk Fell and Pillar, and the Scafells, and the Irish Sea and the Solway Firth are often clearly visible. I can't remember whether the Isle of Man can be seen on the right day or whether the Loweswater or Buttermere fells are in the way, but most of northern Lakeland from St. Bees Head to Helvellyn and northwards to Skiddaw is on view. Only southern Lakeland is hidden.

Buttermere is one of the least spoiled of the principal valleys of Lakeland and two hundred years ago Father Thomas West selected Lanthwaite Hill as one of the most important view-points, or 'stations' as he called them, in the district. He rode up Buttermere, taking notes as he went, for what was to become

the first real guide to Lakeland, and most people would agree
with this choice, if not with some of his other preferences.
Approaching Buttermere from the north you see the mountains
gradually unfolding as you move up the dale, and then there is
the striking view of Grasmoor End rising from the meadows.
This is Lakeland scenery at its very best, and the road under
Grasmoor and Rannerdale Knotts must be one of the finest bits
of unfenced motor road in the district. Too popular, perhaps, in
summertime nowadays with cars parked along every yard of it,
but out of season there is no lovelier place at which to stop and
eat your sandwiches and enjoy the quietude and the mountain
panorama all round.

Grasmoor is the undoubted king of this area—about the
fourteenth highest mountain in Lakeland, but the biggest in the
north-western fells. There may be few mountains in Europe
older than Grasmoor and his neighbours and he will always
remain a principal Buttermere attraction—a burly, red-faced
giant lording it over the lesser heights and guarding, with Melbreak across the water, the entrance to Nicholas Size's 'Secret
Valley'.

Hopegill Head

The red alpine catchfly grows on Hobcarton's shattered crag
high above the massed conifers of Whinlatter—and only, at
most, in two other places in Britain. And the crag and the
flower are the two most noteworthy features of the shapely
mountain above Coledale Hause that many of us have known all
our lives as Hobcarton but which the map-makers insist on
calling Hopegill Head. Hobcarton has a strong local, almost
metallic, ring about it, a good spiky sort of name befitting the
jagged crag, but Hopegill Head sounds too tame and southern.
But when you stand on the summit and look down towards
Lorton in the north-west you can see that the name is accurate
enough for you are exactly at the head of the little valley of the
Hope Beck that flows into the Cocker and eventually into the
Derwent. But the crag itself is Hobcarton and nothing else, no
matter what you might call the summit which is of lesser
importance.

Mind you, I can't guarantee you will find the red alpine
catchfly if you go to Hobcarton. It grows on the left-hand wall
of one of the gullies facing north towards Whinlatter—and
possibly elsewhere on the crag as well—and when you seek it in

high summer, as I have done more than once, you have to search among hundreds of square yards of blaeberry (or bilberry) hanging over the ridges and towers like the greenest of carpets. Viewed end-on from some little distance away the spiky crag can then look rather like a sunken galleon, hanging in slimy seaweed, and rising, prow first, from ocean depths.

A strange, crumbling crag is Hobcarton, quite unlike any other crag in Lakeland. It must be five hundred feet high along most of its curving length of nearly a mile and is the most disintegrating lump of Skiddaw slate in the district. In places the crag has crumbled away into rickety towers and the way the bilberry clings to these places is quite remarkable. Indeed, I would say this is the most luscious bilberry country in Lakeland and the ling grows splendidly, too, on these slaty fells.

It is the rock that grows the bilberry for it crumbles into small scree and soil that proves particularly fertile to this and other plants, and it is also the rock that produces the red alpine catchfly—but in rather a different way. In a reliable book on mountain flowers John Raven writes that the rottenness of Hobcarton Crag is probably due to some potent mineral, and that the catchfly can survive in Britain "only in conditions that are so repugnant to the majority of plants that any severe competition is eliminated". And so the catchfly and the bilberry grow together happily on Hobcarton, the fruit in greater profusion than anywhere else, and the alpine catchfly on this one crag and another high in the hills at the head of Glen Clova in the Highlands. I believe it has also been sighted on Coniston Old Man, of all places, but not for very many years.

Of course, Hobcarton has long been known as the home of this rare plant and about twenty-five years ago the Friends of the Lake District bought 27½ acres of the face of the crag and presented it to the National Trust. Presumably, they did this not only to protect the plant but also to limit the afforestation spreading up from the valley below. The plant grows exactly where a vein of quartz and pyrites outcrops the Skiddaw slate and not very far away, just over the col and underneath the neighbouring peak of Grisedale Pike, is the Force Crag mine where they are winning barytes, so that this area of Lakeland must be particularly interesting to the mineralogist. I'm told that there are also some interesting spiders on Hobcarton Crag —black with reddish tufts on legs and head—but I'm afraid my knowledge of spiders is extremely slight, and I don't like them very much either.

Hobcarton Crag offers nothing to the rock climber, although some climbing experience is an advantage if you go scrambling about looking for the catchfly. But don't trust any holds; nearly all of them are loose.

The summit of the mountain is a fresh, airy place, particularly after an hour's scrambling about in the bowels of the decaying cliffs. On my last visit the air was alive with darting swifts whose ease of manœuvre never ceases to astonish me. Several times I thought I was going to be transfixed by a swooping beak but at the last second, within inches of my head, they always broke off the engagement. The summit is also a favourite haunt of ravens and you can often watch them swooping and soaring above the crag and now and then alighting on the rocky pinnacles. Few people go over Hobcarton, although it is part of a particularly shapely range stretching from the Loweswater area to Braithwaite which makes a fine ridge-walk. During much of the way you have long serrated ridges dropping down to the valley mostly to your right and almost everywhere the ridge is richly clothed in varied plant life. You won't find much litter on these fells but you can often find the seclusion missing from the more popular mountain tops.

A little care may be needed at one point in bad weather. In between the home of the alpine catchfly and the barytes mine there are, or used to be, some of the nastiest holes in Lakeland, most inadequately fenced on my last visit. Anyone slipping into one of these places would almost certainly never come out again and I have wondered more than once how many relatives the sheep cropping the nearby turf have lost down these frightening depths in recent years.

There's a good walk to the top of Hopegill Head from High Lorton and you can also go up from Whinlatter, although much of the way is through the plantations. Another ascent is to follow Hope Beck but most people will probably approach the mountain from the main ridge, either from Grisedale Pike, a shapely height, or Whiteside. My preference is to do the ridge from east to west coming down to Lanthwaite Green and Crummock in the early evening after the splendid view from Whiteside of the coastal plain of Cumberland, the Solway Firth and the Scottish hills—if I'm fortunate with the weather. All this is fine unspoiled hill country and Hobcarton always a worthwhile place to visit.

Causey Pike

The shapely white cone seen in the background of many of the Lakeland winter scenes pictured by the early Keswick photographers is Causey Pike, the distinctive little fell that presides so gracefully over the lovely vale of Newlands. They chose it—as often as not with the still waters of Derwentwater in the foreground—presumably because, from the right angle, it has the sort of shape we associate with mountains, pyramidical and getting steeper towards the top. And also, perhaps, because it holds the snow so smoothly on its steeply sloping sides.

But Causey Pike, it could be argued, is not really very much of a mountain, being merely the first incident on an extremely pleasant ridge, and not even granted the favour of a height on the 1-inch tourist map of the Ordnance Survey. It does, in fact, top the two thousand contour by a few feet—although there's no agreement on exactly how many—but the scant references to the fell in the guide-books are largely confined to remarks that Causey Pike is a pleasant way off the ridge.

Perhaps this little fell, with no hidden mysteries to explore and no real crags or tumbling gills or tarns, is not a very important mountain. But at least it has a personality of its own and its heather-decked summit is one of the happiest retreats I can imagine on a sunny spring day, with not too many folk about.

The most important thing about Causey Pike is its shape and especially the top few hundred feet. There are not many Lake District mountains that carry almost a label on their summits so that you can recognize them from any angle. Bowfell may be one and Pike o' Stickle another, but Causey Pike must certainly be included. Baddeley calls it "Napoleon's Face", but doesn't bother to explain why and, fifty years later, Heaton Cooper delightfully describes the peak as shaped like the bent horn of an old sheep. Occasionally, in winter time, Causey Pike has looked to me rather like the sagging corner of a badly erected ridge tent, which is far from poetic, with Sail, further along the ridge, appearing exactly like its name—a ship's canvas billowing out in the wind.

This best-known view of Causey Pike is not its only identifying feature. When the fell is seen sideways-on the summit appears as a line of wrinkles—a miniature Crinkle Crags or, as somebody has written, rather like the humps of a sea serpent. So that from almost every angle—and Causey Pike seems to have the facility of popping up between all manner of greater and lesser heights—the summit is unmistakable, in just the same way as the rocky pinnacles of Bidein Druim nan Ramh on the Skye ridge, although lower than its neighbours, can always be recognized at a glance.

The last time I walked over the top was on a pleasant sunny afternoon when two of us circled the fells that encircle the Coledale Beck, taking in Sail, Eel Crag, Hobcarton and Grisedale Pike and then threading the leafy lanes back to Stair through the evening shadows. I remember the heather couches on the top of Causey Pike, the lovely, restful view of the surrounding fells, basking in the sunshine, and the warm greens and browns in the winding dales below our feet. And when we had dozed and smoked we continued on our way along the beautifully soaring ridge towards Wandope with the valley of Rigg Beck down on our left climbing up to the little col that looks down to Crummock and Buttermere.

Several times in recent years I've been on the lower slopes of Causey Pike, or down in the lane by Stair, waiting for one or other of the men trying to set up a new twenty-four hours fell record. More than once Causey Pike has been the last peak of all in a very long day embracing between fifty and sixty tops and we have waited anxiously, watches in hand, for the runner and his companions to appear on the summit. Then all at once, we have spotted a figure, no bigger than a matchstick, on the top and then another and another and, within a few minutes, they have been down in the lane and pressing on determinedly, with only a few road miles to the finish at Keswick. Once it was dark when they came over the top, and we first saw their torches, the light pricking the black shape of the mountain as they edged their way down the summit rocks towards the easy run down from Sleet Hause.

Holiday time attracts the visitors to Causey Pike as it is such a straightforward easy walk from Keswick and the views of Derwentwater and the fells are so fine from the top. Which means that if you want the fell to yourself you should go up midweek or out of season. Causey Pike is a typical fell of the 'slate' country, steep sided, smoothly contoured and grassy, but breaking away into little crags here and there. Perhaps there is no finer mountain viewpoint in the Keswick area, no other height so easily attained with so much lake and dale in the foreground and so much mountain spread all around. So I always think affectionately of Causey Pike—one of the shapeliest grandstands in the district.

11

THE FAR BACKCLOTH

(The Northern Hills)

Skiddaw

FAMILIAR old Skiddaw, the mountain that few of us take really seriously, is a grand lump of fell nevertheless, and deserving of much closer attention than we give it. As a background to Keswick it is a noble mountain, the centre of a well-shaped cluster of fells with sweeping buttresses that seem to emphasize the height of the central peak. With its outliers it stands quite alone—save for its proud neighbour, Blencathra—rising steeply from the Keswick plain and the pastures around Bassenthwaite, or swelling impressively from its tumbled foothills in the remote country to the north. It is this comparative seclusion that adds grandeur to the mountain. Skiddaw's features are rarely hidden by other fells and its familiar shape looms bulkily in splendid symmetry from most angles—a dignified, queenly mountain and, with its attendant fells, the most massive piece of uplifted land in the National Park. For Skiddaw and its outliers make up a much bigger mountain mass than the whole of the Scafell range and several times bigger than, say, the Gables. And its summit is only 150 feet lower than the highest land in England.

Skiddaw, therefore, is undoubtedly a big mountain as British mountains go. It is also probably one of the oldest mountains geologically in the country, and was almost certainly the first mountain in the Lake District to be ascended for the view or just for the fun of it. And I cannot think of another 3,000-feet mountain in Britain that is easier to climb.

Our oldest rocks are Skiddaw slates and even the early

map-makers seemed to know about Skiddaw, although they failed to discover other higher and, one would have thought, more impressive mountains. My Robert Morden map of 1680 misses out the Scafells, Helvellyn and most of the other Lakeland mountains altogether but proudly identifies 'Skiddow Hill' with bold lettering, and in approximately the correct position, too. While the early fell-walkers of about two hundred years ago found the gentle slopes of Skiddaw the least frightening of the Lakeland fells, and now and again were able to pluck up sufficient courage to ascend them—occasionally to the very top.

For hundreds of years the summit of Skiddaw was a beacon point—perhaps originally as a warning of raids from across the Border—and every schoolboy has heard how "the red glow on Skiddaw roused the burghers of Carlisle". It is said that after the Battle of Waterloo, Robert Southey, the poet who lived near the foot of Skiddaw, Wordsworth, their families and friends went up the mountain to light a victory bonfire. So that 150 years ago the summit must have been a familiar place and an early guide-writer commented: "Even a lady may safely ride to the top if in the very highest parts someone manages the horse's head."

Yet, despite Skiddaw's great antiquity, its excellence as a viewpoint, and its association with the very earliest days of mountain walking, many people today write off the mountain as a hill of little worth. Because it has no crags for the climber, no exciting ridges and few surprises, and may be ascended with comparative ease by grandmothers and toddlers, too many of us are apt to ignore hoary old Skiddaw.

I'm just as guilty as the rest. After my first stroll up the mountain as a youngster—I think we ran all the way down on a very hot day and had to be revived with much lemonade—I left the mountain alone for about twenty years, preferring to seek out more exciting places. It is the ease by which the summit may be attained that mostly puts mountain people off, and a few years ago the ruins of the old refreshment hut seemed to emphasize the fell's 'tripper' quality. Mrs. Radcliffe rode over the mountain on a pony as long ago as 1794, Bren gun carriers and tanks lurched about its slopes during the war years and motor cars have, unfortunately, been driven to the summit.

All this is discouraging to the simple walker, and so is the width of the highway that runs some distance up the mountain. And yet, two hundred years ago one of the early visitors was so

Hobcarton Crag and Hopegill Head
The ridge to Whiteside from Hopegill Head (overleaf)

alarmed by the view opening out below his feet that he had to abandon the ascent. Another man found that breathing on the mountain had to be performed "with a kind of asthmatic oppression", and later, during a thunderstorm, had the unfortunate experience of watching his guide "lying down on the ground, terrified and amazed". So Skiddaw was regarded with some respect many years ago, and considering that more of England can perhaps be seen from its slopes than from any other place in the country, and pondering on its many other virtues, it is a little unfortunate that we value the mountain so little today.

Admittedly, the easiest way from Keswick to the top of the fourth highest mountain massif in England has few excitements, but this is only one of half a dozen different ways up the fell. Perhaps this was the very first tourist route up a Lake District mountain and tens of thousands of people have gone this way, but on some of the other tracks to the summit you may never meet a soul. Indeed, although the popular side of Skiddaw may be among the most familiar and least formidable slopes in Lakeland the 'back' of the mountain is still almost 'undiscovered'. You can still find plenty of untracked wastes in the 'Back o' Skiddaw' country that John Peel knew so well, and can easily get lost there in bad weather if you don't take care. And the scenery in this little-known part of Lakeland can be invigorating and rewarding—Dash Falls, for instance, and the fine combe of Dead Crags as approached from the road to lonely Skiddaw House. There can hardly be a lonelier place in England than Skiddaw House—two miles due east of the summit of Skiddaw, and at least four miles across the mountains from any other house. Shepherds live there during most of the year, sheltered by a belt of trees that is the only afforestation in the vast stretches of moorland still called Skiddaw Forest. But the lonely Skiddaw hermit lived in a crude, nest-like hut on the lower slopes of Dodd, just above where the late Graham Sutton, the Lakeland novelist, had his home in more recent years. He was called George Smith, and appeared in the district about a hundred years ago painting portraits for a living.

The multiplicity of the valleys skirting Skiddaw and its adjoining fells ensures that the mountain is not one that can be explored in a day or two. Few people can claim to know all these valleys really well, but all of them lead to the summit ridge and each has its own individuality. I don't think there is a finer view in the whole of Lakeland than that looking south and west, into

11

The northern slopes of Skiddaw
Fort on the summit of Carrock Fell
   (*Bowscale Tarn below shadow*) (facing)

Borrowdale and the Lorton fells, from the slopes above Apple-thwaite or even from the lovely Applethwaite road itself. Under snow Skiddaw is a wonderfully impressive sight, and it is also one of the most colourful of the mountains of Lakeland during the summer-time and autumn, because of the profusion of the heather and bracken on its slopes. Geologically, Skiddaw must be one of the most significant mountains in Britain, and although its crags are not especially striking—Skiddaw slate does not make good climbing rock—they do at least have the merit of being tucked out of sight of the casual viewer, and therefore all the more rewarding when sought out by the more discerning.

And yet despite all these attributes, Skiddaw is a mountain that thousands treat with near contempt. But what's wrong with Skiddaw? People will tell you it's too easy to climb and too near the streets of Keswick but there are other ways up if you take the trouble to seek them out, and any Keswick resident will tell you: "It's a grand mountain." And so it is, especially on its northern side. A mountain to be explored and studied on all sides—not just from the 'front': a mountain that can grow on you.

Blencathra

Blencathra, "the hill of the devils", is the finest of the northern peaks of Lakeland, and it seems unfortunate that the fine old British name should have been rejected by many people for the very ordinary, descriptive name of Saddleback. True, its flat skyline has little about it of the traditional mountain shape, but its fine, rocky ridges slanting down to the Threlkeld road, and the wonderful combes scalloped in between more than make up for this deficiency. Indeed, this southern face is one of the most impressive mountain walls in Lakeland and if the fell was this rugged all the way round it could rival the Scafells. But from the 'back'—the lonely northern valleys sloping away to the great Carlisle plain—Blencathra is a slightly disappointing mountain, with little except size and solitude to commend it. Perhaps you could say that Blencathra is a big, broad-shouldered lump of a mountain, with good looks rather than strong character. For all its goods are in its shop window which faces south and east but its summit, once achieved, is something of an anti-climax.

Preferably, therefore, you should study Blencathra from the right angles—and best of all under snow—when it will be seen to be one of the most impressive mountains in Lakeland—as well as one of the biggest. For although there are at least ten Lakeland mountains higher than Blencathra there are not many *bigger* from the point of view of area, and the 1-inch, hill-shaded tourist map of the Ordnance Survey shows the mountain as one of the most massive within the National Park. Norman Nicholson once wrote that if you hollowed it out you would have a dish-cover or soup-tureen that would fit over London. He then went on to reveal, surprisingly, that all the people alive on earth could easily be heaped inside—and indeed, inside even smaller Lakeland mountains—a theory rather difficult to check, but perhaps true enough.

Photogenically, Blencathra stands almost in a class by itself. If you are driving northwards through Lakeland you get your first real impression of the mountain from the top of Dunmail Raise but the full height and magnificence of its splendid southern wall is not really appreciated until you are somewhere near the Thirlmere dam. Hundreds of photographers have stopped spellbound near the entrance to St. John's-in-the-Vale and reached for their exposure-meters and, especially if the mountain is hanging in snow, have been able to obtain dramatic mountain pictures without even leaving the car. And from the Penrith to Keswick road as you approach the mountain from the east there is a view with Scales Fell and Sharp Edge rearing skywards in steepening surges that, under some conditions, can make the mountain look twice as high and steep as it really is. Another splendid view is that of the ridges sweeping down towards Threlkeld and in one of the most impressive Lakeland mountain pictures ever taken W. A. Poucher has shown these under snow, a whole succession of them, so that our modest fell looks like an Alpine giant. While on the mountain itself walkers scrambling up these southern or eastern ridges can obtain striking pictures which could not easily be bettered on mountains of character like Scafell or Gable.

The sun was shining right across the broad front of the mountain as I drove through St. John's-in-the-Vale on a recent visit towards the turn of the year, and the birds were singing by Birkett Bank. Blencathra looked like a great wall of rock, bracken and heather with its ridges slanting down to the plains like the flying buttresses of a cathedral, and the Alpine-like village of Threlkeld, nestling in the sunshine at its foot, reminded me, for a moment, of Innsbruck sheltering below the great wall of the Hafelekar. And, perhaps, the comparison, except in scale, is fair enough, for this side of the mountain rises nearly 2,500 feet in a little more than a mile and is one of the biggest mountain walls, in steepness and area, in Lakeland.

I went up the centre of the wall and straight to the summit cairn, a route that Wainwright, the guide-book writer, describes as "positively the finest way to any mountain top in the district". Admittedly, it is a fine, airy route, but I don't think I would give it the palm; not enough surprises and changes of scenery. My dog and I did it in exactly an hour and a quarter from the main road, including a halt in the heather for it was very warm, so that it is really a very easy mountain to ascend. About a hundred years ago Ruskin went up this way and afterwards wrote enthusiastically: "It's the finest thing I've yet seen, there being several bits of real crag work and a fine view at the top over the great plain of Penrith on one side and the Cumberland hills, as a chain, on the other. Fine, fresh wind blowing, and plenty of crows." I didn't see any 'crag work' but I saw the 'crows'—a pair of ravens I met on the way down Sharp Edge. They rose into the wind and hung quivering in the sky until they turned and dropped into the combe like stones, sweeping back on the wind a moment later, twisting and turning and looping like fighter aircraft.

Despite Ruskin's eulogies Blencathra, unfortunately, has no crags worthy of climbing, although one of the very earliest climbing photographs taken in the Lake District—by the Abraham brothers—shows two people in awkward attitudes, joined by a short rope and, surprisingly, moving together on what appears to be the crags below Sharp Edge. But no climbs have been recorded on the mountain, the rock below the ridges lacking height, continuity or interest.

Blencathra is, therefore, essentially a walkers' mountain and the quicker you walk, if you are going up one of the central ridges, the quicker you get away from the derelict lead-mines with their untidy spoil-heaps that do not weather into the fellside like the debris from abandoned quarries. Compared with these eyesores the railway line on my last visit looked completely innocuous and I watched a train winding past the whitewashed farm houses, the scattered shelter-belts of oak and larch and patchwork fields within their tumbled walls. The hand of Man continues from the valley some distance up the wall until the mountain rears upwards towards the sky, leaving only the top walls of the intake-fields hanging like a chain below the lower rocks. And then, nothing but the bracken and heather.

On the way up on this side you can admire the views down into Doddick Gill and Gate Gill on either side of the ridge—splendidly carved combes encircled by crags with the sheep grazing on the terraces and looking, if you stretch your imagination a little, rather like the kittiwakes perched on the ledges of St. Bees Head. On either side the ridges sweep downwards in smooth lines and then, suddenly, you are at the summit cairn and into the wind on a bare, level ridge. Take a few steps forward and you look out over a different world. Now you are off the ladder and looking out over mile after mile of the beautiful, desolate country known as the "Back o' Skiddaw", the country John Peel and his little Galloway knew so well.

Further along the summit ridge and guarding the eastern approach to the mountain is Sharp Edge, an airy rooftree hung above the black waters of Scales Tarn which provided one of the coldest bathes ever for the two Grasmere men who, some years ago, bathed in every one of Lakeland's hundreds of tarns. Years ago Sharp Edge was regarded as a sensational approach to a mountain summit but, except in high wind or when iced, it is straightforward enough even for the average walker, and should be included in either the ascent or descent if you wish to catch the full flavour of the mountain. Scales Tarn, once thought to be the crater of a volcano and to be bottomless, is, in fact, only about twenty feet deep. Early travellers also described the tarn as a watery abyss upon which the sun never shone and where you could see the stars at noon, which are also claims which can be discounted. Sir Walter Scott wrote some lines about this—although unaccountably getting the mountain mixed up with Glaramara—while another poet gave immortality to two fish said to be living for ever in the depths of Bowscale Tarn, about two miles to the north. This, too, to say the least of it, seems unlikely.

Blencathra has other points of interest—the two quartz crosses laid out on the summit plateau, the long sweeping curve down to the Glenderaterra Beck, the sanitorium on its western shoulder, and its neighbouring outlier of Souther Fell where, it is said, a phantom army was seen more than two hundred years ago. But the principal glory of the mountain will always be the profusion of its splendid ridges reaching upwards to the summit plateau. All should be sampled in turn and the upper combes explored, if you want to know your mountain, while in winter-time skiers who combine the traverse of the mountain with the ascent and descent of neighbouring Skiddaw can enjoy one of the finest tours in Lakeland.

The great tourist tide seems to sweep past Blencathra, and the easy slopes of Skiddaw are ascended far more often than the wonderful ridges of Blencathra, which, for those of us who prefer our mountains to be quiet, may be no bad thing. Skiddaw is Keswick's own mountain, a loftier height and a fell with great beauty of outline, but Blencathra, with its hidden cliffs, rocky combes and soaring ridges is the more rewarding fell to climb. You could spend a week going up and down it in a dozen different ways and still find something new—and perhaps never meet a soul.

Carrock Fell

The first mountain in Lakeland if you come in from the north-east is Carrock Fell—a wrinkled hill of volcanic rock surprisingly stuck on the end of the great northern upthrust of Skiddaw slate. You turn a corner somewhere near Hesket Newmarket and there it is straight ahead—a rather uninspiring dome of grass, bracken and heather. Or you may be on your way to the "Back o' Skiddaw" country from the south or east and, after outflanking the Blencathra range, turn through the sleepy hamlet of Mungrisdale. About a mile or so beyond the hamlet you cross the Caldew and embark upon a delightful unfenced road used as much by sheep as by motor cars. On your left is a tumbled, boulder-strewn slope, studded with juniper and gorse, and the unseen summit above is that of the modest, little mountain of Carrock Fell.

Here is no fine peak, guarded by great crags and buttressed by soaring ridges, but none the less Carrock is a fell of character and rare individuality. For where else in Lakeland is there a mountain with an ancient hill-fort on its very summit, and where else in these parts can you climb on gabbro—the wonderful rough rock of which the Black Cuillin of Skye is made? Indeed, they say that Carrock Fell contains more varieties of rock than almost any other height in England while its southern slopes carry some of the most colourful patches of purple heather in Lakeland, and you can find white heather there much easier than in many parts of the Highlands. Yet an old guide-book—one of the very few to mention Carrock Fell—dismisses the mountain with: "It is not much visited by strangers, nor has it any merits to induce us to recommend such a deviation from the beaten track."

But Carrock Fell is an ideal place to visit when the mists are down on the higher fells, or for a short day, or for a bit of amateur geology or perhaps for a picnic with the children. Just the place for the antiquarian, too. Mostly, however, I have visited Carrock for the climbing—and found the short climbs unexpectedly difficult and much harder than those of equivalent standard in the Cuillin. But we've generally gone on to the summit, or pottered about trying to find old settlements, interesting mine-shafts or rare lumps of rock. For they tell me that even uranium can exist in some of the minerals found on Carrock Fell and the area has certainly been mined for wolfram. You rarely find honest-to-goodness fell-walkers on Carrock. If you see anybody at all they will probably either be climbers trying to identify the rather disappointing little climbs, geologists with hammers, mineralogists or antiquarians. And I once met three young men in the higher crags erecting a hide for bird-photography.

The ruins of the ancient fort on the summit are remarkable. They look like a tumble of large scree, draped in necklace fashion around the highest point but then you see they can't be scree because there are no crags above, and no scree is ever composed of such equally-sized boulders. Many, many centuries ago—I don't think the exact age of the fort has ever been established—men carried these thousands of stones to the summit or dug them out of the ground, and built their fort—perhaps as a lookout over northern Lakeland. Fragments of the original masonry still remain and the ring is broken in several places where perhaps there were gateways. Some distance away from the summit is an elaborate sheepfold built of the roughly-dressed stones from the wall. It has been suggested that the fort could date from the Iron Age, and in this case would be the only hill-fort of its kind in this part of Britain.

But the ruined fort is not the only sign of man's work on Carrock, for on many parts of the fell there are tumuli and artificial mounds—more than two hundred have been noted and mapped—piles of stones, short stretches of wall and sheep bields built perhaps from the collapsed ruins. Archaeologists have not yet pieced together the whole story of this strange little mountain but it seems likely that the early British knew the place and even lived on these heathery slopes above the Caldew. After the earliest settlers or soldiers—perhaps hundreds of years later—came the miners, for down the centuries the fell has been excavated for many minerals, some of them rare. Mineralogists still visit Carrock Mine, more than a mile west of the summit, where wolfram was being worked not so very long ago. And there are other mines not far away, including Carrock End Mine, near the road at the foot of the craggy eastern slopes, and old miners' trods and the remains of watercourses.

All this activity stems from the fact that Carrock Fell is a geological mix-up, due to the sudden ending of the Skiddaw slate and its junction with many different series of volcanic rocks. Geologists can explain this curious mixture, laid down perhaps millions of years apart, but the average visitor can only marvel at the presence of so many different types of rock, sometimes within the space of a hundred yards or so. I've seen lumps of gabbro, granite, slate of various kinds, hard, volcanic rock, and even limestone and sandstone on the same part of the fell, each with their attendant beds of scree and perhaps, not far away, a shining heap of mica quartz. And beneath these piled boulders and jumbled crags the foxes have their borrans—as safe as any in Lakeland. Experts will tell you that some of the minerals found on Carrock are not found anywhere else in England. Various ores containing lead, arsenic and iron are there, and at one time, thirty or forty years ago, there were families living in the villages at the foot of the fell whose fathers had come from Cornwall to work the mines.

From the summit you can see the Scottish lowland hills beyond the Solway, the lonely country at the back of Skiddaw, the Ullswater fells and some of the mountains around Wasdale, the High Street range, the wide expanse of the Eden valley and, behind it, the Northern Pennines—an unusual, if not superb, view. One of its more interesting features, I think, is the sight of Bowscale Fell, just across the Caldew, with the tip of Bowscale Tarn, just visible behind a fold in the fellside. The tarn, rather like Blind Tarn in the Coniston Fells, hangs in a little saucer not far below the summit. If the rims of the saucers are ever broken or washed away both tarns will spill into the valleys.

On my last visit to Carrock the buzzards were soaring five hundred feet above the heather and the sun was glowing on the ruined fort, although the clouds hung low over Blencathra and Skiddaw. There was no sound, not even the chatter of scree or the trickle of water, and it was difficult to realize that men had known these lonely slopes for two thousand years or more. Many years ago an acquaintance of mine excavated one of the tumuli on the western slope of the fell and dug up burnt bones, charcoal and a piece of copper. Probably a burial ground, but could it have been a place of sacrifice? We don't know, and Carrock Fell still keeps its secrets of days before our history was first recorded.

12

AROUND THE RIM

(Some Outliers)

Harter Fell (Dunnerdale)

WHEN I was a youngster our way to the shrine of Wasdale
Head which we thought the most wonderful place in the world
lay over the south-western fells that stand between the central
mountains and the sea. We would start in the early morning,
laden with rucksack and tent, from the railway-station at
Broughton or Foxfield and walk by way of Broughton Mills and
the shoulder of Stickle Pike down to the Duddon. Crossing the
river we would then climb up through the woods to Grassguards,
along the western slopes of Harter Fell, down into Eskdale and
finally over Burnmoor to a favourite camp-site beside the Lingmell Beck. Several times we did this walk in both directions,
often coming down from Grassguards to the stepping-stones
across the Duddon in the darkness, so that we came to know
this side of Harter Fell quite well, but it was a few years later
before we bothered to scramble to its rocky summit to discover
that here was a really splendid little mountain. And yet when
Helvellyn, Gable and the Langdale Pikes are swarming with
people and cars are grinding over Hardnott Pass in scores you
will probably find Harter Fell deserted except for the sheep and
perhaps the buzzards flying overhead. For this little mountain,
comfortably tucked between Eskdale and the Duddon, has never,
to my delight, been a particularly popular shrine. Thousands
drive over the pass within a thousand vertical feet of its summit
each year and maybe hundreds walk along our boyhood route
across its western flank, but not many people scramble to its

three-pronged top and the fell is pleasantly free of highways, cairns, rusty tins and orange peel.

This neglect of one of the western outliers of Lakeland is surprising, for Harter Fell, despite the prolonged activities of the foresters on its eastern and southern slopes, is a colourful, shapely little mountain and a fine viewpoint—a compact, knobbly mass of volcanic rock, splashed with bracken and heather, and now, most nobly ringed with trees. Perhaps only a little hill as British mountains go but an upland of character with a niche in history. For long before the Normans there was some sort of fort at Castle How on the north-eastern skirts of the fell, and for nearly two thousand years the summit has looked down on Hardknott Fort, just over a mile to the north. Almost certainly the Romans or their legionaries will have scrambled to the craggy top where the Ordnance Survey now have their triangulation column, and looked out over the Scafells or westwards down Eskdale to the sea.

Harter Fell may be said to belong to both the Esk and the Duddon since its becks feed both rivers but for me it has always been a hill in Dunnerdale—the best hill in Dunnerdale. Mostly, it has been the perfect hill for a summer evening before the sun dips below the summit—low enough to run up and down after tea with a bathe in the glorious pool at Birks Bridge to round off the day, and ideal for an evening scramble on the crags above the loop in the river. Sometimes we used to take a rope and, avoiding the fellside as much as possible, try to pick out a rock route all the way to the summit. The last time I was on Harter Fell, I had seen no one on the mountain all day until coming down to Birks in the evening. On one of the lower cliffs a crag-fast sheep was bleating piteously and I worked my way across to see if I could do anything although I had no rope with me this time and was encumbered with my dog. But, strangely enough, the only people I saw in the valley that day were climbing on this little-visited crag and, by an odd coincidence, I knew them. When I told them about the sheep some distance above them and to the left, the leader went up to organize its rescue, but no sooner had he poked his face round the corner of the ledge on which she was marooned than the old ewe took her courage in both hands and leaped and scrabbled upwards to safety. She must have been on the ledge for at least a week for every scrap of herbage had been consumed or scratched away but it had taken a strange human face to frighten her into making the move she had been toying with for days. (Which is not to make any criticism of the features of my friend, A. B. Hargreaves, the well-known climber, and would-be rescuer!)

The top of Harter Fell is an attractive place, quite craggy, with the actual summit rather higher than the Ordnance Survey column, a magnificent view of the Scafells five miles away to the north, and a bird's eye picture of Hardknott Fort. Thousands of people drive over the pass each year without noticing the fort, and even from inside the ruins its square shape is not apparent. But from the summit rocks of Harter Fell it stands out—thanks to the labours of the Office of Works—like a town on a map, and must be more visible nowadays than it has been for hundreds of years. You can see where the commandant's house stood, the headquarters block, the granaries and the baths, but you have to know where to look to spot the parade ground— about three hundred yards away to the east on a slightly higher shelf. Here, nearly two thousand years ago about five hundred levies from Spain, France and parts of central Europe were licked into shape by Roman centurions, and here, for upwards of a century, they watched the road through the mountains and down to the sea.

Harter Fell is not the same mountain I knew as a boy but has by no means been ruined by the Forestry Commission. It is part of their Hardknott Forest Park formed about twenty years ago and embracing 7,275 acres between Esk Hause in the north and Grassguards in Dunnerdale to the south, and from Wha House in Eskdale over the passes to the Three Shire Stone. This is among the finest mountain country in Britain, but only about one-quarter of the area is plantable—you can't grow conifers on crag and scree—and much of the suitable land in Moasdale and Wrynose Bottom has been acquired by the National Trust since the Park was formed. All that remains for afforestation are something like 1,300 acres around the lower slopes of Harter Fell and I understand that the present limits of the Commission's operations represent their planting boundaries. Upper Eskdale will never be planted with conifers nor will any more of the central valley heads. And nowhere will the conifers march above the 1,500-feet contour.

The way the Forestry Commission have gone about their job on Harter Fell is most encouraging. The regimentation you see elsewhere in Lakeland has been avoided as much as possible, while skylines have been left clear, and hardwoods liberally planted among the conifers. Sitka and Norway spruce may not be indigenous trees, but neither is the larch which Wordsworth found so offensive but which we now admire as one of our own, like the oak, ash and rowan. The evergreen spruces are also lovely trees—the Norway, with its blunt, dark green needles and the Sitka, almost blue-green or silvery. And with the spruces the Commission have planted on the slopes of Harter many thousands of larches and pines—European larch and Japanese larch and the magnificent Scots pine—as well as the broad-leaved hardwoods. There are beech, red oak and Norway maple, besides Lakeland rowans and birches, so that the woodlands are nearly always charming and colourful. The beech in particular is a most colourful tree—russet throughout the winter, pale green in the spring, a deeper green in summer and then the full glory of its autumn beauty—and the yellowish-green of the Norway maple glows like patches of sunlight among the darker greens of the conifers. The walker, however, has been left his paths through the new forest and while you can hardly now wander at will you may at least reach the summit by a variety of routes.

The map gives no clue to the attractiveness of Harter Fell, for its regular rings of contours suggest no more than a dull, rounded cone, but in reality this is a very worthwhile hill, splendidly alive with colour and shape. Although the mountain is so well-wooded on its Duddon slopes it is a fell where the rock seems to be scratching through to the surface on all sides, and the summit is a wonderfully rocky place, with its three little towers and pretty little scrambles to the separate cairns. Here is a splendid eyrie for a warm summer evening, with fine views of the Scafells and long vistas down the dales and out to sea, and to me Harter Fell is mostly an evening mountain. Perhaps we have watched its shapely form from Eskdale at sunset and seen its colours slowly change from smoke-grey to the purple of evening, or sat on a couch of bilberries looking at the sun going down over the sea, or run down through the conifers to the Duddon for our bathe in one of the best pools in Lakeland.

Black Combe

Some years ago I was incautious enough to suggest in an article —in a picturesque sort of way—that Black Combe being made out of Skiddaw slate, could be among the oldest mountains in the world—and have never been allowed to forget this indis-cretion. Geologists, both professional and amateur, and all sorts of 'experts' on the history of the earth, wrote either to the editor or myself questioning my suggestion while, in the subsequent correspondence, others, perhaps no less qualified, sprang to my defence. It became, indeed, quite a prolonged and intricate controversy about the age of the rocks of which the world's mountains are made, and aeons of time such as 500,000,000 years were freely quoted with great authority, but the issue was never really sorted out. One eminent professor of geology was prepared to go so far as to say that some Lakeland mountains were probably very much older than, say, Everest, while another was equally certain that there are even some Scottish mountains much older than our Skiddaw slate, and others in North America and Africa incredibly more ancient. But it was at least comforting to be assured by all these authorities that Skiddaw slate is very, very old indeed—even to a geologist—and that Black Combe is therefore a very ancient mountain. So there I'll leave it, being careful to make no more claims, for what's a million years to ordinary people?

Black Combe is a familiar mountain, perhaps the most familiar mountain in the Lake District to tens of thousands of people. Many townsfolk who may not know the graceful shape of Great Gable nor the broad shoulders of Scafell Pike nor the massive bulk of Helvellyn know Black Combe, even though they would not dream of scrambling to its summit. They can see it from the sitting-rooms of their houses in Morecambe or from the North Pier at Blackpool or from a score of places along the Lancashire coast—a great sprawling, whale-backed hump of fell standing on its own on the very edge of the sea, a dominating mass of moor and mountain. And I am told you can also see it from the tower of Liverpool Cathedral and even, on a clear day, from the mountains of Snowdonia.

Although Black Combe may be only a small hill in terms of mere altitude—its summit failing by thirty-one feet to reach the magic two thousand-feet contour—it is really much more of a mountain than many higher peaks in bulk and grandeur, in its isolation and in the view from the summit cairn. Was it Wordsworth who wrote that from the top of this modest fell you can get the best and longest view in Britain? And he was probably right. I have heard it claimed that the view from the summit to Jack Hill near Hanley in Staffordshire is the longest continuous overland view in England and it is said that you can see fourteen counties from the cairn if the weather conditions are favourable. Certainly on a clear day you may see from the top, the hills of Galloway in Scotland, the peaks of Snowdonia and eastern

Wales, the Isle of Man and the mountains of Eire, but this is not exceptional for I have seen all these from Scafell. And, since the mountain almost sits on the coastline, you can see Black Combe from ships leaving the Mersey and from the summit often pick out shipping in many parts of the Irish Sea.

During my boyhood I lived almost in the shadow of Black Combe. At any rate that was how it seemed to us for although the mountain was perhaps ten miles away as the crow flies it sometimes seemed no distance away at all and appeared to fill the whole view. We could see the little crags around the combe —we believed as youngsters it was an extinct volcano—the lines of its ravines, the bracken and the heather, and even the farms at its foot. This, we believed, was a bad sign, for if Black Combe was so clear it would probably rain the next day. And there were other days when we could not see the mountain for days or even weeks because of mist and rain, and better days when the sun shone on its snows or the shadows of the clouds raced across its sunlit summit. Sometimes, as we looked at Black Combe across the water, it looked near enough for us to row across in half an hour, and often, from the highest point near my home, we traced the coastline around the Duddon estuary and across the foot of the mountain and watched the smoke of the trains as they chugged along past Green Road.

It was, of course, our first mountain. We didn't know there were easier ways to the top and so we just went straight up from some point along the Whicham Valley road and carried on until there was nowhere higher to go. To a small boy it seemed a very big mountain and I can still remember, although it is more than forty years ago, how we thought we had reached the top three or four times, only to see another even higher lump of fell just ahead. From the summit we looked down on the Furness peninsula spread out below us like a map and then turned round and looked at the Lake District mountains. We did not know it was a famous summit and that Wordsworth had been up there and this would not have excited us if we had. To us Black Combe was just an old friend and we wanted to look out from his shoulders.

On a much more recent visit to Black Combe, showing much less initiative and energy, I drove round it by motor car. We went along the old road over Bootle Fell, nowadays in much better condition than it used to be, and completed the circle by way of the coast road and the road through the Whicham Valley. Black Combe still looked a big chunk of fell—its area is much greater than many higher Lake District mountains—but this time it seemed somewhat lacking in character. The slopes up which I had scrambled as a boy looked steep enough, and the mountain seemed proud and bulky, but not particularly impressive or shapely or exciting. And indeed, Black Combe is really only a mountain of character when seen from afar or when you are enjoying the view from its summit. Wordsworth believed its 'dread name' to be derived from the clouds and storms which often beset this exposed outpost, but he was being much too fanciful. Other people have traced the name to the dark heath with which its western side is clothed, but almost certainly the name refers to the black combe, visible from miles away, on the south-east slopes below the summit.

As we drove over the old road across the back of Black Combe we looked down on the tall chimneys of the atomic energy station towards the north-west, but it seemed easier to look back into the past. This is an old smugglers' road, but the history of these parts goes back much further than a few hundred years and, indeed, fades away into distant dark days which may always remain a mystery. Perhaps we will never know the meaning of the ancient stone circles, old burial-grounds and relics of strange rites practised long before history began. Men, they say, came to the back of Black Combe from the continent in the Bronze Age and perhaps earlier, and today you can still see the signs they left behind. Long before the Celts there was a village on these bleak moors and scattered around are burial cairns and even the remains of fortified positions.

Most Lakeland lovers have heard of the Swinside Circle, only half a mile away from a good road, but hardly anybody takes the trouble to go there. And there were once at least five other stone circles in the same neighbourhood, although few of the stones remain. Black Combe is also a mountain of the fairies, and is said to have its own hobgoblin who would do your work for you if you put out for him a bowl of porridge, well laced with butter. They also used to say that the bees sang at midnight on the fell on Christmas Eve, and that you could always forecast the weather in advance by the way the cattle lay down.

But today, as you bump along this ancient road through a deserted countryside of a long-forgotten age, there is little to remind you of the past. Black Combe may be a very ancient mountain indeed and the old stones full of meaning, but a Herdwick nuzzling in the bracken and a curlew hopping across the stony track bring you back to the fun of being about in

Summit crags of Harter Fell above Dunnerdale

Lakeland on a sunny day, not far below the clouds. And that's
how I like to think of Black Combe—an ancient outpost guarding Lakeland from the sea, but a pleasant, breezy upland where
you can escape the crowds and look out over half of England.

The Howgills

Although the Howgills are outside the Lake District National
Park they are essentially part of the Lakeland scene. I see them
every day from my home near Kendal—a familiar shape, suggesting sleeping elephants, spread across the eastern horizon—
and the traveller along the Windermere to Kendal road cannot
fail to notice, from somewhere near Ratherheath, the line of
sculptured beauty straight ahead. While the visitor coming from
London by rail sees them towering above him as the train
swings into the Tebay gorge.

And yet, although so many thousands of people see these
splendid fells every summer weekend, very few bother to
explore them. I don't think I've ever met another walker when
wandering along the Howgills, and there are very few tracks up
there. If you are really seeking solitude this is one of the few
areas where you are certain to find it.

The Howgills must be among the least-known of the many
groups of fells in the north-west. They are vaguely accepted as a
pleasant backcloth to many scenes but are not even identifiable
by name to the vast majority. They stretch from Sedbergh to
Tebay, east of the Lune and the railway, and lie mostly within
that corner of Yorkshire that bites deeply into east Westmorland. I often used to think that Westmorland would be a much
more compact and neatly shaped county if the boundary em-
braced all this fine fell country but nowadays boundary changes
hinge on much more practical matters than scenery. As it is, the
boundary lies along some of the tops of the Howgills leaving
most of the area in Yorkshire, although Westmorland claims
Langdale Fells—a much lonelier country than the famous Pikes
—as well as Tebay Fell.

There's nothing for the climber in the Howgills but for the
walker or the skier it is superb country—clean, lonely hills with
just a few sheep about, buzzards and larks, an occasional
tumbling beck, plenty of fresh air all round, and views full of
blue sky and sunshine. From the summit ridge on a clear day
you have an unusual view of the Lake District mountains, and
identification, from this unusual angle, may be difficult, while

12

Winter in the Howgill Fells

to the north, over High Street, there is Crossfell in the Northern
Pennines and, in the opposite direction, the whole length of the
Lune, stretching down to Morecambe Bay.

Potentially, the Howgill Fells are the best ski-ing country
in the north of England. They are smooth and rounded, grow
little or no heather, carry no stone walls and sport few crags and
screes while the fell grass needs only a slight covering of snow
to be negotiable. Against these advantages, however, must be
set the misfortune that these hills, being relatively low, attract
much less snow than the higher Lakeland fells. Each winter,
when viewed from the west, they appear—especially when the
sun is shining—to be plastered with snow but upon closer
examination the covering will often be found to be inadequate,
even for these accommodating slopes. In addition, the best
slopes face west and south-west, catching the warmest sun, so
that the snows have to be quickly seized before they disappear.

But often in the Lakeland area we have freak snowstorms
with winds blowing the snow away from places where it is
normally deposited and plastering it on western slopes and in
the roads. And these are the days when we go ski-ing in the
Howgills—days of sunshine and snow and blue skies and mile
after mile of perfect scenery spread out below. We have sat up
there in our shirt-sleeves in February eating our sandwiches and
looking down on the main London to Glasgow railway-line.
Every now and again a diesel express, or sometimes a slow
freight train, would go rattling through the gorge and we could
see and hear engines shunting and watch men, like ants, working
on the line. Sometimes we would look down into the lovely
length of Borrowdale—nothing like so well known as its Cumberland namesake, but a pleasant, peaceful place none the
less.

The traverse of the long range from Sedbergh to Tebay, in
either direction, could make one of the finest ski-ing expeditions
in the country, although a non-ski-ing motorist would be needed
to pick you up at the far end. One day I went on skis from the
farm at Carlingill at the foot of Black Force to the highest point
of the range—The Calf (2,220 feet)—and back, and I have done
other sections of the ridge on ski at different times. Boys from
Sedbergh School know the southern fells in the range, particularly the slopes of Winder, better than most people and Cautley
Spout, round 'the back' of the Howgills is a tourist attraction—
the only one in the area.

Cautley Spout is not a hidden waterfall, like several in the

Lakes, but lies in full view of the main road and from the fields all around—a torrent of water precipitated down the fellside in three leaps from a height of eight hundred feet into a dark pool below. It makes a fine picture, especially after heavy rain, and you can start your traverse of the range from here if you wish to shorten the Sedbergh to Tebay route.

Perhaps winter is the best time for the Howgills, either on foot or on ski, because then the views are much more dramatic, but in summer-time it is a wonderfully restful countryside and, as the late Sir Clement Jones once wrote: "Wherever you look in the Howgills everything is composed and in the right spot and there is nothing to jar." I can find no reference to the Howgills in the usual guide-books but in one interesting volume, *The Old Hand-knitters of the Dales*, there is a beautifully accurate description of them. "Near Sedbergh," the book states, "the Howgill Fells, hump-backed hills as sleak as sealskin, reflect the sunlight like shot-silk." Norman Nicholson, however, thought the range looked like a row of mud pies.

Sometimes, when approached from the Grayrigg road the Howgills give an impression of massive sculpturing that you don't often get in the Lakeland hills, except perhaps on Blencathra. They seem to react to the play of the sunlight and shadow much more than do less smoothly shaped mountains and this light and shade or modelling is especially noticeable under snow. Indeed, I have known days when the Howgills, draped in snow from top to bottom and lit sideways by strong sunlight to expose the gashes of their shadowed gullies have seemed, at a distance, not unlike some great Alpine range.

Undoubtedly, then, this is splendid country to look at from the car or train but much more rewarding if you take the trouble to walk up the slopes of Winder and on to The Calf or leave the Tebay highway at Low Borrowbridge and wander along the county boundary towards the Kirkby Stephen road. So that the next time you find Lakeland choc-a-block with motor cars and people and you want to get away from it all, turn away to the east and go exploring in the Howgills. I don't think you'll be disappointed.

Cross Fell

If you look at a map of England that shades the mountains over two thousand feet you will see that the biggest mass of high land in the country is not in the Lake District but in the

Northern Pennines. The Scafells, the Helvellyn range and Skiddaw are higher, but if you lumped all these fells together, top to toe, you would still not have achieved the vast bulk of the great mountain barrier that lies to the north-east of Appleby. There can be few places in England more remote than this bare, windswept plateau from which the horizons, east to west on a clear day, must be up to 120 miles apart, and a man might spend weeks up there without meeting a soul. The highest summit of the range is called Cross Fell and for many years it was considered the highest mountain in England. At one time it was believed to carry patches of eternal snow.

This sprawling backbone of the Northern Pennines would be magnificent walking country were it not so bedevilled by tussocks and peat hags but it can still be a rewarding skyline to visit for the strong goer who knows how to use his map and compass and is not afraid of bad weather. For Cross Fell gets much more rain and snow than most Lakeland mountains and the winds up there are legendary. The immense base upon which the mountain and its attendant heights stand is nearly thirty miles in circumference and you can walk for twelve miles along the plateau without dropping below the 2,000-feet contour. And you can't do that in the Lake District without doubling back on your tracks.

The Northern Pennines, unspoiled as yet by 'progress', are always a welcome change from the more popular hills and in winter-time especially have their own particular charm. You can go for miles in these hills and never see a tree or a house or even a sheep and perhaps very few birds. And clustered around the feet of these remote hills are some remarkable towns and villages—Alston, the highest market town in the country, Dufton and Milburn, with their wonderful village-greens and historic farmhouses, Long Marton, with its fine old church, and Knock, pressed right up against the fells. Hereabouts you see the red sandstone in the roadside walls and houses, the finest stone of all for showing its colouring in the winter sunshine.

From the summit of Cross Fell you look west towards the pastoral beauties of one of the most pleasant, fertile and restful valleys in England—the Eden valley—and east towards the wild, windswept moorland of Durham and the upper Tees. Sometimes the contrast is remarkable. You may often, in winter-time, see the sun smiling in the Cumberland fields nearly three thousand feet below and glinting here and there on little streams, or the windows of distant farmhouses. But eastwards the view may be of mist and cloud hanging over dreary, snow-flecked moors that fall away in miles of bare desolation towards the dark shadows of the industrial north-east.

One curious feature of the mountain, setting it apart from most others, is that from the summit you can see almost nothing —nothing except less than a quarter of a mile of dull foreground and then the limitless sky. The reason is that Cross Fell rises very gradually from the plains that surround it until, a short distance from the summit, it suddenly steepens into a sort of collar of rock that encircles the mountain. And from the top of these rocks the actual summit is seen, only a little distance away across the gently rising plateau. During most winters, following the snows and the thaws, this top cap of Cross Fell— above the collar of rock—remains a glistening, white dome while the snows on the rest of the mountain have deteriorated into patches and drifts.

Cross Fell is 2,930 feet high, which means it is higher than Pillar, Fairfield, Blencathra and most of the Lakeland mountains. It lies in Cumberland but the Westmorland boundary crosses the range by its southern shoulder and the Durham boundary is lower down its eastern slopes. When first seen from the Appleby-Kendal road near the top of Orton Scar—or even from the Shap to Penrith road—Cross Fell is the left-hand and the highest of the three distant summits, and is often snow-capped during some winter weeks when the Lakeland hills from the south appear to be bare. The middle summit is Little Dun Fell and the right-hand one Great Dun Fell. On a clear day you will be able to pick out the masts of the radar station on this last-named summit, reached by the highest road—private in its upper parts—in Britain. Several times each winter we go into these fells for the ski-ing and I have many happy memories of sunlit afternoons in the snow, but also of other days of storm or ice or mist with winds so strong that sometimes we could hardly stand. One of the good days was once when we skied to the summit of Cross Fell along rippled snow, hard as ice, in dazzling sunshine but against a biting wind. But on the return journey, with the wind at our backs, we sailed for a mile or more along the plateau, quite effortlessly as if we had little engines on our skis. The only sound was the gentle hiss of the thin planks sliding over the snow and the flapping of our anorak hoods about our ears.

Few, if any, English mountains retain their snow longer than Cross Fell. More than two hundred years ago the geographer

George Smith went up the mountain in the middle of August and was surprised not to be able to find even "the least relicks of snow in places most likely for it". Nowadays, we know it is most unlikely that Cross Fell could ever retain snow so late and the only place in Britain where there is eternal snow is in one corner of the Cairngorms where tiny patches may always be found in August and September. In the eighteenth and nineteenth centuries, however, snow was sometimes said to linger throughout the year on the highest Lakeland hills. Perhaps our winters are becoming milder. A traveller, 180 years ago, reported drifts on Cross Fell clearly visible from Penrith halfway through June—which is not really very remarkable—but he added that in places the snow remained throughout the year. The scientist John Dalton wrote about finding snow on Helvellyn in July "in the usual place", just north of the summit, on several occasions during last century.

More people have heard about the Helm Wind—the mountain's own wind—than have ascended Cross Fell, although the only difficulty about the ascent is caused by the negotiation of its weary peat bogs, which are particularly trying when filled with soft snow. The Helm Wind is a violent, cold wind that sometimes causes great damage in the Eden valley. It has uprooted trees, blown the roofs off houses, and even overturned horses and carts and its roar can be like the sound of an express train. The wind is often characterized by a thick bank of cloud resting along the Cross Fell range and a parallel section of cloud known as the Helm Bar. The phenomenon is probably caused by a cold, wet wind blowing up the long eastern slopes of the range and meeting the warmer western air of the plateau.

There are no tourist tracks to the summit of Cross Fell, so far as I am aware, and no cairns, apart from the heap near the survey column marking the highest point, but here and there are tracks sideways across the slopes made, not by sheep, but by workmen of a hundred or two hundred years ago. Indeed, despite the extreme desolation of the mountain, you will find, in a score of places, if you look about you, evidence of the hand of Man. For hundreds of years men have mined for lead and other minerals on these slopes and you can see how they have diverted the becks or sunk their holes or strewn their spoils. Cross Fell may be a proud, lonely mountain today but many years ago it must have been a busy place. And it remains a mountain of individuality—perhaps not the highest mountain in England, as the map-makers used to think, but probably the biggest in bulk and certainly one of the most remote and least-visited. Here, on the summit plateau of this mountain of the wind and the snows, is the perfect grandstand from which to view the distant glories of the Lakeland fells.

INDEX